HURRICANE

A FIGHTER LEGEND

HURRICANE

A FIGHTER LEGEND

John Dibbs and Tony Holmes

Foreword by Air Commodore Pete Brothers

First published in Great Britain in 1995
by Osprey, an imprint of Reed Consumer Books
Limited Michelin House, 81 Fulham Road,
London SW3 6RB and Auckland, Melbourne,
Singapore and Toronto

ISBN 1 85532 498 9

Written and Edited by Tony Holmes
Page design by Paul Kime
© Cutaway drawing by Mike Badrocke

Printed in Hong Kong

Acknowledgements

The authors would like to thank Bill Bedford, Pete Brothers and Clive Denney
for sharing their various experiences, and photographs, the Fighter Collection
for making G-HURI available for aerial photography, Mike Stroud for
selected proof reading and photographs, Ken Ellis for selected factual
accuracies, and the following individuals for providing photographs; Duncan
Cubitt, Jeremy Flack, Luigi at Hulton-Deutsch, Phil Jarrett, Michael O'Leary,
Richard Riding/*Aeroplane*, Mike Vines and Richard Winslade.

Front and back covers Nick Grey enjoys himself at the controls of Hurricane
XIIa G-HURI at medium altitude above a thick cloud bank over Duxford in
October 1994 *(John Dibbs)*

Title Page As the Hurricane celebrates its 60th birthday in 1995, the
airworthy survivors of the breed can be counted on one hand. Of this elite
band of Hawker fighters that still feel the wind beneath their slab wings on a
regular basis, this marvellous machine is probably now the most flown of the
lot. G-HURI, alias Canadian Car & Foundry's Hurricane Mk XIIa c/n 72036
(RCAF serial 5711), has been a most welcome participant at many airshows in
both the UK and Europe since September 1989. Part of Stephen Grey's
burgeoning Fighter Collection stable, G-HURI was photographed in its
element over Duxford during a flight specifically arranged for this book in
October 1994 *(John Dibbs)*

Right As this work is specifically a celebration of the Hurricane in its
airworthy state, this is the only shot within the volume of a Hawker fighter
parked away in a dusty museum corner. Part of the large RAF contingent
within the Brussels Air Museum, Hurricane IIc LF345 was one of five or six
(both figures have been quoted) of the type transferred to the Belgian Air
Force from the RAF's Metropolitan Communications Squadron in 1946. Used
as both hacks and high-speed communication aircraft, the history of this
particular machine is open to some conjecture as its serial belongs to a
Hurricane written off near Booischot on 2 July 1947 whilst serving with No
169 Wing! It also wears totally spurious code letters, which actually reflect its
call sign when in service with the Belgian Air Force *(Jeremy Flack)*

For a catalogue of all books published by Osprey Aerospace
please write to:

**The Marketing Department, Reed Consumer Books,
1st Floor, Michelin House, 81 Fulham Road, London SW3 6RB**

Contents

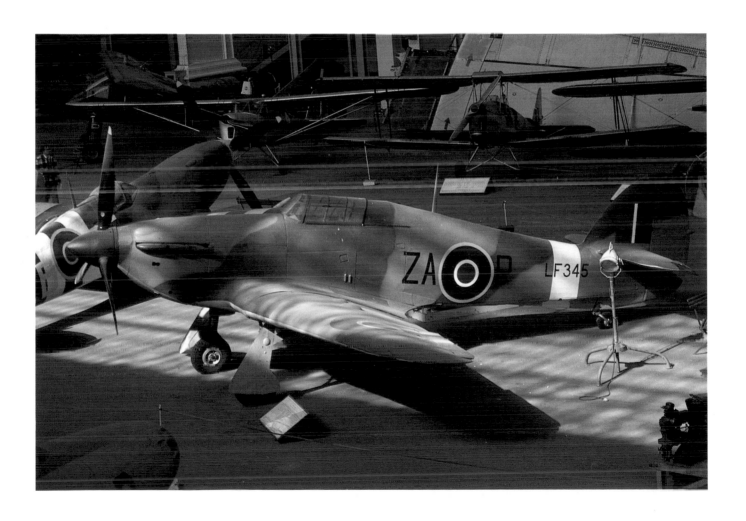

Foreword

The date was 24 September 1938. The place was RAF Biggin Hill. My excitement was intense for today I was to fly Hurricane L1655, the first of No 32 Sqn's long awaited replacements for our Gloster Gauntlet biplanes.

Having studied Pilot's Notes I climbed into the cockpit and sat for a while finding my way around the levers and switches, then started up and taxied over the grass – we had no runways – to the boundary, turned into wind and took off. The big two-bladed wooden propellor gave surprisingly rapid acceleration, whilst the throaty roar of the Merlin and the solid, rugged, feel of the aircraft as it bounded over the uneven surface stimulated and inspired confidence. Retracting the wheels, a novel experience, involved moving the left hand from throttle to stick and select wheels up with the right hand and depressing the pump lever until the wheels locked up. As this loss of throttle control made formation take-offs unusually interesting we later surreptitiously attached a Bowden cable from the stick to the lever to avoid the hand change. Now airborne, I closed the canopy, another novel experience, and relieved of the head-buffeting slipstream of an open cockpit, settled down to enjoy myself.

Having climbed to a safe height I tried a variety of aerobatics and was delighted by the immediate and smooth response to the controls. When stalling the aircraft I was interested to note that the right wing dropped, a Sidney Camm characteristic I had found common in other aircraft he had designed. On landing from this 50-minute 'Type experience' flight I looked forward with exultation to the future, and the opportunity to get to know the Hurricane really well.

So it was on the outbreak of war a year later that I was in the enviable position of thoroughly knowing its advantages and limitations, and was looking forward to the opportunity of testing it in battle. By now we had progressed from de Havilland two-pitch metal propellers to constant-speed Rotols, much improving performance. Proof that I was a Hurricane pilot of experience was available for all to see, for the lower right leg of my trousers bore the customary Hurricane glycol stain!

During the lull in activity after Dunkirk we flew some night patrols, but here the Hurricane was out of its element for the exhaust flames streaming down each side of the cockpit did not enhance night vision. Moreover, as initially we were allowed no airfield lighting, finding the airfield and landing by use of the headlights was fraught with interest. Although adjustable downwards, the beams converged under the nose so the tree through which I flew was totally hidden from view. But this sturdy aircraft, festooned in branches, merely shuddered, and being of pedigree stock was little damaged.

This book, with its beautiful photographs, is more than a collector's item. It has been most thoroughly researched, to such an extent that I have learnt hitherto unknown details of actions in which I was involved. Finally, it at last does justice to the Hurricane as the stalwart, indomitable, trusty fighter and joy to fly it was, and provides a reminder that it was the backbone of Fighter Command in the Battle of Britain when Hurricanes shot down more enemy aircraft than all other defences, ground and air, combined.

P M (Pete) Brothers, CBE, DSO, DFC*
Nos 32 & 257 Sqns, 1940

Right Few photographs depicting the hectic summer months of 1940 embodied the irrepressible spirit of Fighter Command better than this one of Flt Lt Pete Brothers, taken on the day he downed a JG 51 Bf 109E over Kent, and thus became an ace – the date was 29 July. It was just one of many shots compiled by a Fox Film Unit sent to Hawkinge airfield, near Folkestone, with the set purpose of making a series of instructional films for the RAF (*via Pete Brothers*)

'Blue Peter'

BATTLE OF FRANCE

Twelve pairs of eyes squinted out in all directions as the Hurricanes steadily climbed on patrol beneath a thin layer of high cloud. They must have made an impressive sight from the ground, all stacked up in tight 'Battle Formation' in the best traditions of the pre-war RAF. However, this was no longer an environment conducive to pageant-style flying routines, perfected in the peaceful skies of southern England during endless squadron drills.

Their audience, if indeed they had one, consisted of bewildered civilians streaming towards the channel ports of Calais and Dunkerque. In their midst, the remnants of the rapidly disintegrating British Expeditionary Force (BEF) were attempting to hold a dangerously mobile enemy along the border between France and Belgium. Lacking supplies, up to date information and a co-ordinated defensive plan shared with their French allies, the shell-shocked army regulars barely noticed the four vics of Hurricane Is that comprised No 32 Sqn as they droned on overhead.

At 10,000 ft the chaos below was barely discernible to a fresh-faced Flt Lt Pete Brothers, who kept a watchful eye on the remaining members of his vic, as well as scanning the flat landscape ahead of him. Like the other 11 pilots strapped into their Hurricanes, Brothers was anxious to test his mettle against the marauding Luftwaffe, who seemed to be avoiding his squadron at all cost. Across the broad battle front that stretched from Rotterdam in the north to Nancy in the south, motorised columns of German troops swept across the plains of the Low Countries, supported in their Blitzkrieg tactics by *Luftflottes* 2 and 3.

Most other Hurricane squadrons committed to the defence of France – either based on the continent with the Air Component of the BEF or on daily rotation across the Channel from bases within No 11 Group – had, by this stage, experienced combat to varying degrees. Some, like Nos 1 and 87 Sqns, had been all but wiped out by the end of the first week of Blitzkrieg. No 32 Sqn's war up to this point (18 May) had, by contrast, been very low key. The unit had been performing a tiresome routine of pre-dawn launches from Biggin Hill that saw them making landfall at bases in France, or Belgium, at first light. From there they were given orders to

Above The caption for this original Hawker publicity shot could have read 'First of the Many', or 'One down and only 14,532 to go', with the benefit of barely a decade's hindsight. When it made its debut flight on 6 November 1935 from Brooklands airfield in Surrey, K5083 was the equal of any fighter that had, up to that point, taken to the skies. Sleek, shiny and unencumbered by a radio aerial, gun ports or a larger production-standard radiator bath, the Hawker Monoplane F.36/34 prototype looked the part with its big wooden Watts propeller, driven by the 1029 hp Rolls-Royce Merlin C engine. Flown initially by Hawker's Chief Test Pilot, Flt Lt P W S 'George' Bulman, this machine was only christened Hurricane on 27 June 1936. That same month the Air Ministry announced an order for 600 of the type. K5083 survived the rigours of test flying at both Hawker's Langley airfield and the RAF's test establishment at Martlesham Heath, following which it was finally grounded and turned into an instructional airframe *(via Aeroplane)*

patrol a certain section of the Franco-Belgian border, or perhaps escort a flight of Battles or Blenheims as they attempted to stem the flow of Wehrmacht tanks and troops flooding into the heartland of France.

Once their mission had been accomplished, the weary pilots would recover to whatever base they could find. Here, they would individually refuel their own Hurricanes using small tins of gasoline and a hand-pump, with a chamois leather serving admirably as a filter. The squadron would depart almost as swiftly as they had arrived, returning to a pitch-black Biggin Hill at around 11pm.

This routine had been strictly adhered to for almost a fortnight, and 'Blue Peter' – his nickname due to him being flight commander in charge of 'B' Flight– was beginning to think that he would never cross swords with the much-vaunted Luftwaffe. Little did he know that rapidly approaching his battle formation at roughly the same altitude were several *schwarmes* (roughly 18 aircraft) of Bf 109E-3s of I./JG 3 *Udet*. On this fateful day No 32 Sqn had been tasked with escorting Blenheim IVs on a raid that would take them past the town of Douai, whilst elements of I.*Gruppe* had been given free rein to patrol the region in search of Allied aircraft. By this stage the Advanced Air Striking Force had been reduced to a handful of light bombers, and the Hurricane squadron failed to find any Blenheims to escort. Unperturbed, they boldly pressed on in a north-easterly direction, confident that their impeccable 'Battle Formation' would ensure their invincibility.

Heading the formation was Sqn Ldr 'Baron' Worrall, who had barely been with the unit a fortnight. Checking his compass and watch in one sweeping glance, Worrall decided that he had led his squadron far enough into uncharted territory, and was on the verge of wheeling the formation around back in the direction of the Channel when a cluster of small black specks appeared on the horizon. Due to the closeness of the vics, several pilots spotted the ever-growing dots virtually simultaneously. Amongst the ranks of the eagle-eyed was Pete Brothers. Sensing that his time had at last come, he activated the reflector gunsight fitted to his Hurricane and the familiar symbology appeared on the glazing in front of his eyes. His fingers ran over the safety catch on the paddle grip of the control column, switching the gun ring to fire, whilst his eyes made one final check of the instrumentation. After four years of training Brothers was ready for the impending clash.

As the Hurricanes rapidly closed on their quarry, the black dots quickly assumed a more tangible appearance, until in the fleeting seconds prior to the two formations merging it became crystal clear that these were indeed Bf 109Es. Sqn Ldr Worrall did not deviate from his course, and more than two dozen fighters somehow flew through each other in opposing directions at over 300 mph without a single head-on collision taking place. Brothers snapped his head up in time to see a blue/grey Bf 109E hurtle overhead, the appearance of its oil-streaked cowling still vividly etched in his memory 55 years later.

'Good God, that's the enemy!', he exclaimed to himself, and quickly reefed his fighter around to see in which direction the Germans had flown. Like No 32 Sqn, the I./JG 3 pilots were also pulling into hard turns in order to gain an advantage over the violently manoeuvring Hurricanes. Brothers soon fixed his sights upon a single Bf 109 that had lost altitude as it had turned back to rejoin the battle. He levelled off and closed on the German

Above The great man behind the Hawker legend, Sir Sydney Camm, CBE, FRAeS. Director of Design at the company for almost five decades, he was responsible for arguably the greatest continuous line of fighter designs the Western World has ever seen. Born in the shadow of Windsor Castle on 5 August 1893, Camm joined the H G Hawker Engineering Company in 1923, and remained loyal to the firm until his death on 12 March 1966. He was knighted for his services to British aviation in 1953
(British Aerospace via Bill Bedford)

fighter, whose pilot soon realised that he was being stalked. As the Hurricane closed to within firing distance, its target began to gently jink, vortices streaming off the wingtips of the Messerschmitt as the *jagdflieger* desperately tried to shake off the trailing fighter before its pilot had a chance to open fire.

Throughout the brief chase that lasted just a matter of minutes, Brothers could think of only one thing – a rather incongruous piece of advice given to him, and the rest of his intake at RAF Uxbridge some four years earlier by the legendary World War 1 ace, Sqn Ldr Ira 'Taffy' Jones, which was made all the more memorable due to the fact that the latter stuttered quite badly. 'There's going to be a f, f, f. . . ing war, and you chaps are going to be in it. I can give you one p, p, piece of advice. When you get into your f, f, first combat, you will be f, f, f. . .ing f, f, frightened. Never forget that the chap in the other c, c, cockpit is twice as f, f, f. . . ing frightened as you are!' Now fighting for his life, just as Jones had predicted, Brothers therefore thought to himself, 'this chap must be having hysterics so I'd better put him out of his misery'.

He promptly took aim, allowed for a little deflection, and opened fire. The Bf 109 was quickly set alight and it crashed in a ball of flame in an open field near Maubeuge, only a matter of miles from the Belgian border. Brothers' first thought was that his actions must surely have been seen by other I./JG 3 aircraft in the immediate vicinity, and the downing of a comrade would have no doubt infuriated them somewhat! He felt sure that they would be after him in pretty short order. A further two Bf 109Es had been despatched by No 32 Sqn pilots in the brief melee that marked their introduction to aerial combat in World War 2.

Thinking it wise to beat a hasty retreat away from the smouldering wreckage of his vanquished foe, Flt Lt Brothers quickly plotted a course for Merville on his battered RAC motoring map – flying charts for France were rare for British-based squadrons. By the time he popped over the hedge at the BEF airfield west of Lille and set his Hurricane down after a straight in approach to land, his neck was aching severely. Brothers had spent the entire 15-minute duration of his 'escape' performing non-stop contortions in the cockpit to ensure that his tail was clear of avenging Bf 109s. The jubilation of this, his first combat kill, quickly subsided when he realised that he would have to single-handedly refuel his thirsty fighter and make tracks back to England.

Hurricane Mk I N2524 finally touched down on home soil and taxied back to its perimeter dispersal at Biggin Hill at 10.45pm, where its dedicated flight sergeant immediately set about draining the remaining gallons of fuel from its tanks – this was a regular ritual performed after each and every sortie in late May 1940 as the fuel used in France was only 90 octane, and was therefore too lean a mixture for the Rolls-Royce Merlin to run on for extended periods of time. Prior to leaving his machine in the capable hands of the groundcrew and heading off to the mess for a spot of supper, Brothers ensured that his motor car had had its tank filled with French fuel – there was no point in wasting it!

BATTLE OF BRITAIN

By 24 August 1940 a battle-weary Flt Lt Pete Brothers struggled to remember what peacetime flying felt like. Gone was the sense of frustration at hearing on the radio and reading in the newspapers of the success that other Fighter Command squadrons were enjoying in fleeting skirmishes with the Luftwaffe. The Battle of Britain was now technically entering its third phase, which saw the Luftwaffe targeting RAF fighter stations primarily in No 11 Group. However, to the pilots of No 32 Sqn it was just another day of frenetic and bloody dogfighting over south-east England.

Scrambling two or three times a day from either Biggin Hill or, more frequently, from their forward base at Hawkinge, near Folkestone, the squadron had been in the thick of it for almost two months solid. Since the beginning of July they had lost 16 Hurricanes in combat, but quite miraculously had only had a single pilot killed. Six of these aircraft were destroyed in a single day (18 August), three repelling a low-level raid on Biggin Hill at 1.00pm by nine Dornier Do 17s of 9./KG 76, and the rest in the late afternoon countering raids against the Medway towns. Again the squadron was fortunate, with only one pilot suffering serious wounds.

The morning of the 24th dawned bright and clear. Over the previous four days, the exhausted pilots of No 11 Group had enjoyed a respite from the vicious airfield raids that had hit virtually every station in the south-east. At Biggin Hill, No 32 Sqn had received no less than eight replacement Hurricane Is since the bulk of their force had been lost six days before. Finding a similar number of experienced aircrew to fill the cockpits of

Right Looking considerably more war-like than the prototype Hurricane, L1547 was the first production standard fighter of its type and made its maiden flight at Brooklands, where this shot was taken, on 12 October 1937. Considering the revolutionary layout of the Hawker fighter, its powerful eight-gun armament and its relatively untried powerplant, a span of barely two years from first prototype to production aircraft was a truly remarkable achievement. Steadily upgraded to full Hurricane I specs during the first 12 months of the war, this machine was finally lost on 10 October 1940 whilst assigned to the Speke-based No 312 (Czech) Sqn when it suffered a major engine fire during a training flight. Although its pilot, Sgt Otto Hanzlicek, bailed out he subsequently drowned when he landed in the River Mersey (*via Aeroplane*)

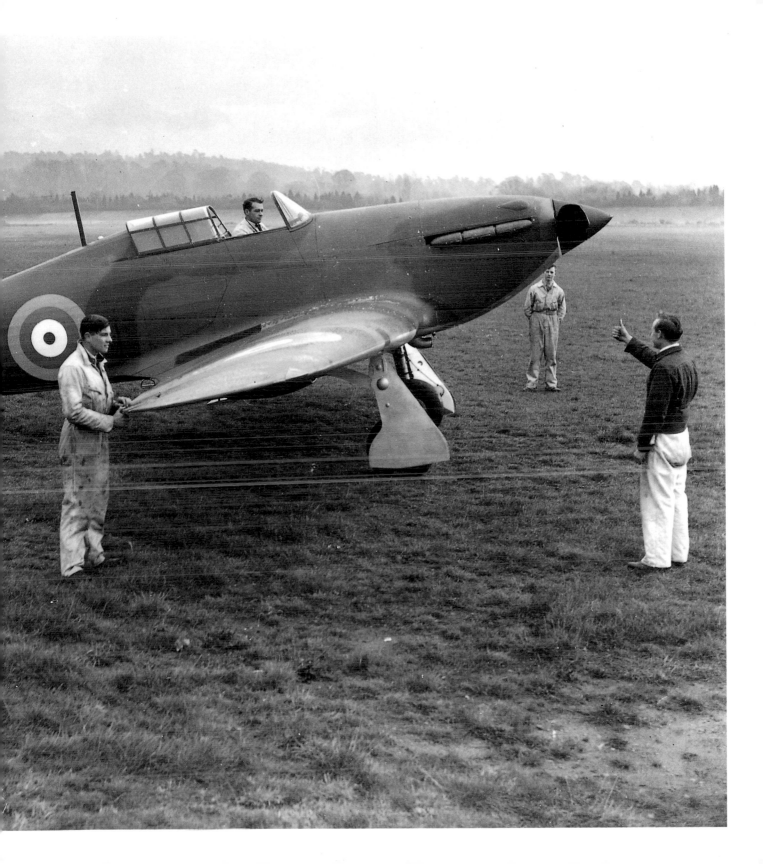

these machines was a far harder task. Fortunately, the unit still had two veterans from France at the helm, namely acting Sqn Ldr Mike Crossley, known to all and sundry as 'The Red Knight', and Flt Lt Pete Brothers. Both were to be heavily involved on this sunny Saturday in late August.

Brothers had enjoyed a remarkable degree of success in aerial combat since his first brush with the Luftwaffe three months earlier, his score standing at nine kills confirmed up to this point. However, as he is at pains to point out today, the thought of having achieved the status of ace never crossed his mind at the time – survival was far more important.

The Luftwaffe launched their first raids at around 8.30am, massed formations of Ju 88s and Do 17s, escorted by large numbers of Bf 109s, hitting targets in a broad band across the south-east. Many squadrons were scrambled in an effort to break up the tightly packed bomber formations, but the escorts performed their job well, and few raids were stopped. No 32 Sqn had risen early and departed 'The Bump' at 5am, flying down to its forward station of Hawkinge where it was kept at readiness. There they watched fellow Biggin Hill-based No 610 'County of Chester' Sqn, equipped with Spitfire Is, wade into a far larger formation of fighters and bombers on a late-morning raid on Dover.

From their vantage point on the hills above the Channel ports, they could see contrails in all directions, with the smoke from several large fires to the east marking the position of successful raids on the battered Dover docks. By early afternoon No 32 Sqn got the word to stand down again as the Luftwaffe returned to its airfields in France and prepared for the traditional second wave of attacks that would arrive at around 2.30pm. Brothers and his colleagues knew that they would be sent out to tackle the 'afternoon shift'. With time on their hands, many pilots took advantage of this lull to give their aircraft a quick once over prior to the inevitable order to scramble.

'GZ-L', alias P2921, was the personal mount of 'Blue Peter', and it wore a small blue flag beneath the cockpit to the port side as proof of its 'ownership'. This Hurricane I had been one of three Hawker fighters delivered to No 32 Sqn on 11 June 1940 as attrition replacements for the unit following their escapades over France. It was allocated to Brothers on 3 July, and served him well for the rest of his time at Biggin Hill – P2921 was the only one of the trio to survive the Battle. Always serviceable, this machine was never once hit by enemy fire whilst in the hands of Pete Brothers.

It was no ordinary Hurricane either, having been modified by its pilot, with the help of his flight sergeant, in order to gain a few extra mph. The standard issue external rear-view mirror, bolted on to the canopy framing, had been deleted, and a curved car-type mirror fitted internally in its place, whilst the dozens of proud sitting rivets that covered the wings had been systematically filed flat during quiet moments on readiness. 'The combination of the mirror and the rivets produced a fair amount of drag, and by removing both we added at least 5 mph to "Blue Peter's" top end speed, and thus created the fastest Hurricane in the squadron', Brothers proudly remarked when interviewed for this book in late 1994.

As predicted, the afternoon raid was detected forming up over the Pas de Calais soon after 2.15pm, and by the time No 32 Sqn received the order to scramble, the mixed formation of 40 Ju 87B-1s and 60 escorting Bf 109Es, had Dover in their sights. This particular raid was highly significant for several reasons, not least of which was the fact that it marked the final appearance of the much-vaunted Stuka in British skies during the Battle. An icon of the Blitzkrieg, the Junkers dive-bomber had suffered terribly at the hands of Fighter Command just six days before when no less than 16 Stukas from the three *Gruppen* of St.G 77 were lost in 10 minutes of sheer hell over the Isle of Wight. A massed raid had been staged to knock out the radar sites at Poling, Ford and Thorney Island, but the lightly escorted Stukas had run headlong into a large defending force of Spitfires and Hurricanes and the unwieldy dive-bombers paid a heavy price.

St.G 77 was stood down to lick its wounds, joining St.G 2 who had suffered a similar fate two days previously during a daring raid on Tangmere, on the Sussex coast. By 24 August only St.G 1 had sufficient aircraft left to mount an attack in strength on the channel coast, and it was the dark green Stukas of II. and III.*Gruppe* that now sallied forth once again towards Dover, their progress being monitored from several thousand feet above by elements of JGs 3 and 51.

The low pitched din of 40 Junkers Jumo 211Da engines droning over the Channel at 15,000 ft was still well out of earshot to the pilots of No 32 Sqn who sat around in the hot afternoon sun at Hawkinge. Although it may have looked a relaxing scene to the casual observer, all 12 aircrew knew something was brewing out to the east, and although not a word was exchanged about the impending sortie, each pilot understood what was required of him. At 2.20pm the telephone rattled to life in the dispersal tent and shattered the seemingly endless silence. The dreaded, yet for many relieving, sentence of 'Squadron scramble', was shouted for the umpteenth time that summer by the duty airman, sending the pilots off on a Le Mans-style sprint to their awaiting Hurricanes.

By nature individualists, fighter pilots adopted different techniques to speed up their departure from terra firma, and Pete Brothers was no exception. He believed that a simple, no-nonsense, approach to strapping in was the key, and to achieve this he always ensured that his parachute was fitted into his cockpit prior to clambering aboard. Then, it was just a matter of fastening the harness once in, waving away the trolley accumulator and opening up the throttle.

Aided in his pre-sortie preparations by an ever-willing groundcrew, Brothers was rolling out to take-off across the cratered Hawkinge strip in a matter of minutes. He quickly glanced in his mirror as the speed built up and the bumps evened out, and was gladdened to see two other members of Blue Flight, Irishman, Flg Off Rupert Smythe, and Pole, Plt Off Karol 'Cognac' Pniak, racing along on either side of him. Both pilots had become aces with No 32 Sqn in the past weeks, and both would be shot down within the hour over the Channel ports.

Brothers firmly applied back pressure on the control column as the Hurricane reached take-off speed and the fighter willingly departed Hawkinge. Now began the seconds of feverish, yet totally co-ordinated, hand movement repeated at this same juncture by every Hurricane pilot the world over, which saw the undercarriage and flaps retracted through the manipulation of the relevant lever, situated slightly aft of the incumbent to his right hand side in a H-shaped gate arrangement. This tricky procedure could only be performed by the pilot using his right hand, which therefore meant that for a few seconds straight after take-off he had to maintain control close to the ground in a reasonably tight formation with his left hand. 'You could always tell when a Hurricane pilot was "cleaning up" his machine as it tended to porpoise whilst being flown by the "throttle hand". Some pilots mastered the technique of seamless flight with both hands, but most tended not to bother!', Brothers observed decades later.

As the 12 Hurricanes steadily climbed out over Folkestone, the 'Red Knight' quickly checked over the R/T to ensure that the No 32 Sqn pilots had all got off successfully, and once this had been ascertained, he

Right Another splendid Fox shot showing the daily routine of No 32 Sqn at Hawkinge on 29 July 1940. Despite the dreadful losses sustained by Fighter Command's 31 other Hurricane squadrons, Pete Brothers' unit suffered relatively few casualties, as this photograph bears witness to. Of the seven pilots shown here lounging around at dispersal, only one, Plt Off Keith Gillman, was lost during the Battle – he fell victim to Bf 109Es over the Channel on 25 August 1940. The pilots in this photo are, from left to right, Plt Off Rupert Smythe (shot down and badly wounded on 24 August 1940 having scored six kills); Plt Off Keith Gillman (one victory); Plt Off John Proctor (nine kills); Flt Lt Pete Brothers (12 kills in 1940, and 16 in total); Plt Off Douglas 'Grubby' Grice (five kills); Plt Off Peter Gardner (seven kills in 1940, and 8.5 in total); and Plt Off Alan 'Shag' Eckford (8.5 in 1940, and 9.5 in total). Notice that the Hurricane in the background is plugged into the starter trolley in preparation for a short notice scramble, which was the norm for No 32 Sqn when forward deployed to Hawkinge from their home station at Biggin Hill *(Fox Photo via Hulton-Deutsch Collection)*

instructed them to join up prior to intercepting the as yet unseen enemy. Crossley then awaited instructions from Hawkinge fighter control. He didn't have to wait long.

'Jacko Red Leader, this is Sparrow Control. Vector 090, Angels 20. Bandits 100 plus. Buster.'
'Ok, Sparrow Control. Angels 20. Any friendlies to look out for?'
'Yes, Jacko Red Leader. Hornet Squadron joining from Manston. Twelve-strong. Out.'

This short, yet revealing, conversation between Crossley and his fighter controller crackled through the headsets of all 12 pilots, spelling out a big raid. The only support on offer to No 32 Sqn in their quest to blunt this rapidly approaching attack was a single squadron of Spitfires, forward deployed to the all but bombed out Manston from Hornchurch, in Essex. 'Hornet Squadron' was, in fact, No 54 Sqn, a unit that had seen much action since its first patrols over the Dunkirk beaches in May. Led by pre-war flight commander, Sqn Ldr James 'Prof' Leathart, No 54 also boasted the deadly Kiwi duo of Flt Lt Al Deere and Plt Off Colin Gray within its ranks, the latter having already claimed a Bf 109 earlier that morning during yet another raid on Manston. However, like No 32 Sqn, the unit was near breaking point through exhaustion, having lost many experienced pilots in the bloody battles off the Kent coast earlier in the month.

Fires were still burning in Dover as the Hurricanes continued to climb out over the Channel. Brothers had activated his reflector sight soon after take-off, and his thumb fiddled with the gun ring in anticipation of the action which was soon to commence. Someone shouted out 'Bandits.

Right Viewed from another angle, the photographer has obviously said something to tickle the group's collective fancy. In the background, with a parachute harness draped over the tailplane ready to be strapped onto its pilot's back, is Hurricane I P3522, the personal mount of Plt Off Rupert Smythe. He used this machine to shoot down three Bf 109Es (two on the same day) and a single Do 17 bomber, all of which fell in the Deal-Dover area. One of three Hurricanes delivered to the unit at Biggin Hill on 20 May 1940 as Battle of France attrition replacements, this aircraft was hit by fire from a Do 215 off Selsey Bill on 18 August whilst being flown by Sgt Bernard Henson (who was later shot down and killed some three months later by Adolf Galland whilst flying with No 257 Sqn). Its Merlin wrecked by the Dornier gunner's well-aimed burst, P3522 force-landed at Tangmere, where it received a quick engine change before returning to Biggin Hill. There it was crated up and despatched to a civilian repair unit for a thorough overhaul *(Fox Photo via Hulton-Deutsch Collection)*

Left The signal to scramble was phoned through to the No 32 Sqn dispersal soon after the series of relaxed pilot shots were taken. In this panoramic view of Hawkinge the various aircrew can be seen individually preparing for take-off. The pilot of 'GZ-T', which is parked to the left of the picture, is just doing up his parachute straps, whilst his counterpart at the tail of 'GZ-B' has only just reached his fighter and is yet to pull on his 'chute. To the right of this machine, another pilot strides purposefully across the grass to a Hurricane parked out of shot, whilst a fourth young aviator sprints towards 'GZ-K', doing up his leather helmet straps as he goes. This latter Hurricane (P3679), with Sgt William Higgins at the controls, had earlier been shot up by Staffel Kapitan Hptm Horst Tietzen – a Knight's Cross holder and both Spanish Civil War (seven kills) and Luftwaffe experten (27 kills) – of II./JG 51 on 20 July 1940 in an action over Dover that had also seen another No 32 Sqn pilot (Sub-Lt George Bulmer) shot down and killed by II./JG 51 ace Josef 'Pips' Priller, and unit commander, Sqn Ldr Worrall, forced to crash land at Hawkinge after combat with Obfw Ilner, also from II./JG 51.

Horst Tietzen was later killed off Whitstable on 18 August 1940 when he was shot down by Plt Off Pawel Zenker, a Pole flying with No 501 Sqn – the latter was lost six days later north-west of Dover. Sgt Higgins went on to become an ace with five aircraft destroyed (including a Bf 110 on 20 July and a Bf 109E 1 of 9./JG 51 on 24 August, both in P3679) and one shared, before he too was shot down and killed by Bf 109s over the Isle of Sheppey on 14 September whilst flying with No 253 Sqn. P3679 continued to fight on with No 32 Sqn until it was damaged in a flying accident at RAF Baginton on 24 October 1940, and sent to a civil repair unit for overhaul. The pilot running away from the camera in this photograph is more than likely Bill Higgins *(Fox Photo via Hulton-Deutsch Collection)*

Angels 10. Tally-Ho', and just as Brothers was about to dive into the attack having spotted the Stukas already commencing their near vertical dives on Dover Harbour, he heard another, more frantic, call. 'Bandits. Angels 20. Break Red and Blue Sections. Break!'

He reefed his Hurricane around in a tight climbing turn just in time to see a Bf 109E shoot down past his left wing. Scanning the sky for more fighters, Brothers immediately spotted a group of 12 flying in a wide circle above the diving Ju 87s. His section of four Hurricanes were still with him despite the violent evasive manoeuvre, and he immediately signalled his intentions over the R/T. 'Ok Blue Section. Let's join the party below us.' He then dived headlong into the middle of the circle and pulled into a high-g turn behind two yellow-nosed Bf 109Es of III./JG 3.

Pressing the fire button in short bursts, Brothers opened up with his eight .303 machine guns, but failed to register visible hits on either fighter. A quick glance in the mirror revealed a potentially fatal sight – the all yellow nose of another Messerschmitt blotted out the sky behind him. Instinctively, he kicked the rudder pedals at the same time as he opened the throttle, yanking the column hard over to port and back into his stomach. The Bf 109 could outdive both the Spitfire and the Hurricane, so Brothers stood the fighter on its tail and climbed away; this manoeuvre had served him well in the past, and once again did the trick against his erstwhile foe. Sqn Ldr Crossley had watched this brief encounter from outside the circling Bf 109s, having failed in his attempts to fight his way into the enemy formation.

Continuing to climb, he turned in the direction of Herne Bay. Constantly checking his mirror, he mentally noted the absence of his flight, which made him all the more diligent in keeping his rear quarter scanned for signs of the enemy. As he passed through 15,000 ft he spotted a lone Bf 109E-4 cruising along above him. At the controls of the yellow-nosed Messerschmitt was a Lt Achleitner, who had been separated from his *Gruppen* in the initial attack on No 32 Sqn. He had departed his airfield east of Boulogne almost an hour before and was on the verge of returning back across the Channel when Brothers attacked. Without having to rush his aim, the Hurricane pilot unleashed two deadly bursts of machine-gun fire on the now weaving Bf 109, but his last ditch manoeuvring was in vain. Large chunks flew off the fighter's starboard wing, and realising that the damage was terminal, Achleitner rolled the fighter on its back and bailed out – he was soon fished out the Channel by the Herne Bay life-boat.

Running low on both fuel and ammunition, Brothers flew directly back to Hawkinge. He could see more dogfights raging near Dover, as a second wave of Ju 87s swooped down on the harbour. He quickly joined the pattern at the small field, checking his tail the whole time as he lowered the undercarriage and flaps – with his fighter appreciably slowed and

Above An incoming raid of Ju 88s and He 111s was detected by the coastal radar network whilst the Fox man was still out on the airfield on 29 July, and he immediately went over to the closest Hurricane and recorded this electrifying moment for posterity. Plt Off Smythe had sprinted the short distance across to his fighter and clambered aboard with the minimum of fuss. With the starter trolley pulled away and the engine burbling with its familiar throaty note, the Irishman waited patiently whilst the remaining members of B Flight complete their respective pre-flight routines. Pete Brothers led a group of very successful pilots throughout the Battle, all of which had benefited from advice given to them by their flight commander.

When dealing with bomber formations he told them that 'the urgent thing was to get at the bombers before they dropped their bombs, and if you were short of the height you wanted to carry out a stern or beam attack, the best thing to do was take them head-on and go straight though the formation. I always dived underneath the bombers short of impact because I always thought that

the instinctive thing for pilots to do was pull up rather than push down when faced with collision, and the last thing I wanted was to meet a Dornier or Heinkel at close quarters. This manoeuvre also produced additional speed, thus enabling me to pull the Hurricane tightly around once clear of the bomber formation and quickly turn back into them again for a more conventional stern attack.

'Head-on shots were the easiest of the lot to perform because there was no deflection needed whatsoever. I would press home the attack until I thought a collision was almost inevitable. In many respects this was the best form of attack as most bombers had less protection from both guns and armour at the front, although it was very often difficult to confirm whether you had inflicted mortal damage to an aircraft after a single pass, as once you had turned back into the bombers the formation had often scattered in response to your initial assault. With a stern attack you would usually look to set an engine on fire, thus denoting some success for your endeavours' *(via Phil Jarrett)* 'dirty', he made a juicy target for a marauding Bf 109. Picking a spot seemingly free of filled-in craters, the pilot put P2921 firmly down on the grass, slid the hood back and taxied over to a refuelling point where a bowser would soon meet him. Across the field, the familiar 'GZ'-coded Hurricanes of No 32 Sqn were either already on the bowsers, or wheeling in overhead, moments away from landing.

Once his aircraft was chocked, Brothers cut the engine and three airman immediately descended on his fighter. As he paused to take breath, the gun magazine panels were unfastened and removed to allow the armourers to feed in the fresh belts of tracer and Armour Piercing Incendiary that now lay draped over the trailing edge of each wing. Standing alongside the pilot on the port wing, a jocular airman connected the refuelling hose from the back of the bowser, and then proceeded to give Brothers a running commentary on the battle taking place a few thousand feet above them.

A No 54 Sqn Spitfire had, just at that moment, succeeded in administering a fatal blow to a diving Bf 109E, and as the clutch of Hurricane pilots sitting tethered to the bowser craned their collective necks upward, the airman on *Blue Peter* shouted out above the din, 'Good, we've got one.' Barely had these words been uttered, when the *jagdflieger* departed company with his doomed fighter, now hurtling earthwards, and successfully deployed his parachute. Seeing this unfold before his very eyes, the young airman turned to Brothers with a look of absolute disgust on his face and growled, 'The jammy bastard.'

Less than ten minutes after touching down, P2921 coughed back into life and taxied away from its temporary dispersal, followed by the remaining nine Hurricanes. Pilots departed in ones and twos, climbing back out over the Channel to rejoin the battle, and contact was soon made with a group of 15 Bf 109Es, again from JG 3, within sight of Folkestone. Possessing a height advantage once again, the German fighters made a single pass through the lose gaggle of Hurricanes, sending three spiralling out of formation trailing smoke and glycol, the life blood of the Merlin engine.

Amongst the trio of aircraft that fell away was the Hurricane flown by Sqn Ldr Crossley, who stayed with his machine as long as he could before undoing his straps, rolling it onto its back and baling out when the white smoke emanating from his engine turned to black, streaked with red flames. Not a million miles away, Plt Off Karol Pniak couldn't believe his misfortune at having to bale out twice in one day, the Pole having been shot out the sky only a hour or so before after following Brothers into the formation of circling Bf 109s off Dover. Finally, Plt Off Eugene Seghers, formerly of the Belgian Air Force, braced himself for a landing in the sea off Folkestone, a local life-boat watching his progress as they raced out to pick him up. All three would eventually return to No 32 Sqn over the next few days.

The remnants of the unit, meanwhile, claimed two probables as the Bf 109s beat a hasty retreat back across the Channel, with six Hurricanes in hot pursuit. Realising the futility of the chase, Brothers ordered the squadron to 'knock off' the pursuit and return to Biggin Hill. Within 30 minutes the 'camouflaged', sand-coloured, hangars of the famous fighter station hove into view and the squadron joined the landing pattern in ones and twos.

Despite No 32 Sqn having only been scrambled to intercept the afternoon raids, the unit now had few remaining pilots that were fit for flying, either psychically or mentally. Having survived to land back, and invariably enjoyed some degree of success whilst in battle, was enough to keep the adrenalin flowing, and excited discussion and comparison over what happened to each individual now took place. It was only after the squadron stood down that reaction set in, and lack of interest in the morrow was apparent. 'How long can this go on and how long can I last?', was the unspoken thought in all minds. 'We are so few and they are so many.'

It was obvious to all that No 32 Sqn were now a spent force. Indeed, after performing a late afternoon interception the following day, and losing a further two Hurricanes and a single pilot killed to Bf 109Es of I./JG 54, the squadron received orders to fly north to the No 13 Group station at RAF Acklington. At the time of their departure, No 32 Sqn was the top scoring fighter unit in the RAF, with 102 confirmed kills.

For Flt Lt Pete Brothers, his period of rest and recuperation lasted just under two weeks as his experience as a flight commander was urgently needed at a badly knocked about No 257 Sqn. The daily routine of being shaken awake before dawn, at readiness as the sun rose, and scrambling into the massed ranks of the enemy just as most of the civilian population of Britain were sitting down to tea and toast for breakfast, would continue unabated for 'Blue Peter' well into late November 1940. Although he may indeed have been 'One of the Few', his feats of bravery were many.

Right This famous shot was taken by the official RAF Biggin Hill station photographer on the afternoon of Thursday, 15 August 1940 – the day that witnessed the largest ever assault by the Luftwaffe on Britain. Over 1800 aircraft struck at targets in five waves, confusing No 11 Group's fighter controllers as to which raids were genuine as opposed to feint attacks. No 32 Sqn fell victim to the Luftwaffe's ruse and were scrambled north to intercept a handful of Bf 109s of 5./JG 51 that had completed their escort mission and were sprinting for home. Engaged over Harwich, the Luftwaffe pilots were loath to fight due to a shortage of fuel, but nevertheless one turned on 'Grubby' Grice and shot him down in flames. A single Bf 109E-4 was claimed in return, although its conqueror, Plt Off Boleslaw Wlansowolski, in turn had to belly land nearby after his engine seized due to running the Merlin in full boost for too long. The survivors returned to Biggin to refuel and rearm, before being scrambled south this time to Selsey Bill, along with 140 other Spitfires and Hurricanes. They were part of the largest Fighter Command formation that had so far been assembled to repulse the Luftwaffe.

No 32 Sqn waded into the 300+ bomber formation as it closed on Portsmouth, Sqn Ldr Crossley soon sending two Ju 88s down into the Channel with engines ablaze. The rest of the unit quickly exhausted their ammunition and broke off the engagement and returned to Biggin, minus Sgt Henson who had recovered at Tangmere with a seized Merlin. The propeller blades had barely stopped spinning on the nine remaining Hurricanes at the squadron dispersal when the gun covers over the wings were levered off and the refuelling filler caps prised open. The well rehearsed groundcrew had the unit turned round in under ten minutes. Within an hour the squadron was zooming over the grass at the airfield and racing skyward into a holding orbit at 5000 ft over Biggin, listening for further instructions. They didn't have to wait long. The fifth, and last, raid of the day had just hit Croydon airport virtually unopposed and were now heading east to effect their escape. No 32 Sqn travelled right past them into sun before wheeling back around and diving on the Do 17s and Ju 88s. Those extra few seconds spent gaining the tactical advantage served the Hurricane pilots well, as in the ten minutes that the unit were engaged with the enemy, nine fighters and bombers were claimed destroyed – three Do 17s, two Ju 88s and four Bf 109Es. All nine exhausted, yet exhilarated, Hurricane pilots returned safely to Biggin, three of them being featured in this photograph *(via Phil Jarrett)*

The Hawker Habit

Pilots of note often seem to gravitate towards the products of one particular manufacturer during their careers. For example, Jeffrey Quill will always be linked with the fighters of Supermarine, John Cunningham to the varied designs of de Havilland and Roland Beamont with the RAF's pioneer jet fighters and bombers from English Electric.

Another distinguished aviator who slots quite comfortably into this category is Bill Bedford, the world's pioneer V/STOL pilot, and a true Hawker devotee. Between 1941 and 1967, he flew most types of aircraft designed by Sir Sydney Camm and built in the famous Kingston-upon-Thames factory. From the Cygnet and Hart through to the Hunter and Harrier, Bedford mastered them all during an astounding career which saw him ably fill the role of Hawker's Chief Test Pilot from 1956 to 1967.

His first introduction to a Camm design occurred some 15 years earlier, however, when, as a raw pilot, he was posted to RAF Hullavington and No 9 Service Flying Training School, in Wiltshire, for training on the Miles Master and then conversion onto the most famous Hawker type of them all, the Hurricane. Thus began a special relationship with the fighter that was to last until the late 1960s, with Bedford making a particular point of flying Hawker's own Mk IIc PZ865, better known as *Last of the Many!*, right up until his retirement.

The following interview, which took place in October 1994, charts Bill Bedford's lengthy association with the Hurricane from his early experiences at the advanced flying school, through operations in India and Burma to the heady days at Hawkers in the 1950 and 60s, when his flights in PZ865 truly epitomised the term 'joy riding'.

'I arrived at my advanced flying school at Hullavington in 1941, and in a few weeks had accumulated 24 hours on the Miles Master – a type not too dissimilar in appearance from the Hurricane – under my belt. The Hawker fighter had already earned a formidable reputation from the summer of 1940, and as a young man, with the government providing me with a high-performance aircraft in which to hone my skills, it was a privilege to fly the Hurricane. Its Battle of Britain top scoring achievement inspired us all.

'So it was with some considerable respect that I climbed into the cockpit of Hurricane I P2565 (an ex-No 607 Sqn machine that had served

Right Soon to set off on a great adventure from which only a handful of them would survive, the pilots of the recently-formed No 135 Sqn pose for a group shot at RAF Honiley in front of one of their well-used Hurricane IIas. This shot was taken in mid-September 1941, the squadron having only been formed the previous month at Baginton under the command of Battle of Britain ace, Sqn Ldr Frank 'Chotah' Carey. Seen seated here immediately above the port oleo, Carey had scored close to 20 kills up to this point in the war, and was recognised as one of the best Hurricane combat pilots in the RAF. Just to prove his ability with the Hawker machine in any theatre of war, Carey went on to down at least seven Japanese fighters and bombers over the jungles of Burma whilst leading No 135 Sqn against an overwhelming number of enemy aircraft in early 1942 *(via Bill Bedford)*

throughout the Battle of Britain) on June the 18th, 1941, and was thoroughly briefed by my instructor, Flg Off Barry Barnet, who was himself an ex-Battle of Britain chap who had been badly wounded in the arm by a cannon shell whilst flying a Fairey Battle. Having strapped in, I steadily worked over the cockpit and instruments, checking that everything was as it should be according to the pilot's notes. I was immediately fascinated by the split stick with its spade-handle circular grip. In the 10 o'clock position was a brass knurled ring, with a prominant spring-loaded button in the middle that seemed to attract one's thumb like a magnet. This was the gun firing button – the *raison d'être* of this killing machine.

A label adjacent to this device said "SAFE" or "FIRE", and knowing for certain that the guns were unloaded, and ensuring that in any case the Hurricane was not pointing at anything that may take offense, I selected "FIRE", aimed my gunsight at an imaginary Hun in the sun, closed the range to 50 yards, aimed at the top of his fin and pressed the button for two

Left World War 2 saw the RAF combating a wide variety of Axis threats both in the air and on the ground, and although the Hurricane was considered obsolescent in its designed role as a day fighter from early 1941 onwards (particular on the Channel front), it served tirelessly as a ground attack aircraft right up until VJ Day. A youthful Flt Sgt Bill Bedford's No 135 Sqn was one of the Hurricane stalwarts on the Burma front, utilising Mk IIb/cs in the fighter-bomber role from February 1942 through to May 1944, before transitioning onto the ultimate multi-role machine, the Thunderbolt. Illustrating the versatility of the rugged design, this personalised Mk IIc was attached to one of the six Hurricane squadrons still using the Hawker fighter on a daily basis over Burma in the last year of the war, although to exactly which one has never been fully ascertained! What is known is that the armourer on the left was a Leading Aircraftsman R Finney from Hounslow, in Middlesex, whilst his companion, also an LAC, was W Jones from Birmingham. They were photographed at a forward strip in central Burma in May 1945 (*via Aeroplane*)

to three seconds. I "felt" the shudder of the guns "firing" and broke away violently, but not before I saw the flaming Bf 109 despatched on its terminal dive. Walter Mitty Bedford had chalked up his first kill!

One permanent impression that has stuck with me from those days was the vital instruction to trim the aircraft with full starboard rudder bias prior to take-off. This was deemed essential to offset the swing on take-off produced by a combination of the rotation of the propeller, the slipstream, and the gyroscopic effect of the aircraft as the tail came off the ground. The longitudinal trim, by contrast, was set in a near neutral position.

'The next most important thing to do in the cockpit was to have the friction nut on the throttle tightened. If this basic, and rather odd, requirement hadn't been carried out correctly, soon after take-off, when you had to change hands and fly with your left hand whilst engaging the gear up lever from within the combined H-shaped flap/undercarriage selector gate, the unrestrained throttle would come back to the closed position and the aircraft would lose height just when you really didn't want it to. Many a pilot was caught out like this, their aeroplanes being seen to porpoise up and down as they fought to tighten up the nut in mid-air, whilst trying to retract the gear and control the Hurricane with the same hand. Worse still, some pilots subsided ignominiously back to earth with the undercarriage only partially extended.

'The layout of the H-gate was relatively straightforward, but its positioning was not, being tucked away to the right hand side of the cockpit, parallel with the seat. One half of the gate controlled the

Above By the spring of 1944 the Hawker factory at Langley was coming to the end of the long-running production line that had churned out the bulk of the 14,500 Hurricanes delivered to the Allies the world over. It was decided that a single airframe should be earmarked as the 'Last of the Many', and its progress through to completion be photographically recorded for posterity. PZ865, a standard four-cannon Mk IIc, was chosen to be the last airframe – several people who worked at Langley at the time believe that a handful of Hurricanes were built from spares left over at the factory after this machine was completed! This panoramic view of the factory floor was the first to show the suitably decorated PZ865 under construction. In this shot, two tradesmen are securing the primary frame torsion wires near the tail of the skeletal Hurricane. Behind the imposing factory shelter (under which vital tools, jigs and spares were buried), the last batch of Mk IIcs are having their Merlins checked over prior to being rolled out for flight testing (*British Aerospace via Mike Stroud*)

undercarriage up/undercarriage down, and the other flaps up/flaps down. Prior to start-up we would select flaps down, and then by operating the emergency hand pump, check that the latter dèvice worked. The lever was then centred within the gate once these checks had been completed.

'Allied to the undercarriage control was a spring-loaded catch that prevented you inadvertently selecting gear up whilst on the ground, so before take-off you had to ensure that the catch had been released, thus allowing you to retract the undercarriage once airborne. The whole idea of having the gear selector positioned on the right hand side of the cockpit really was a strange piece of ergonomic design, as logically it should have been sited on the left near the throttle gate. However, many other aircraft of this generation were so designed. This layout was just accepted in those days, but would never be tolerated today.

'Happy that the flap/gear selector was in a neutral position, you would

Left No doubt built not too long after *HELLZAPOPPIN* at Hawker Aircraft's Langley works in Buckinghamshire, the 14,533rd, and last, Hurricane rolled off the assembly line and straight into history in July 1944. Looking remarkably similar to the Battle of Britain Mk Is that had streamed out of the same factory four years before, PZ865 appeared old in its design philosophy when compared to the Fighter Command types of the day like Hawker's own Tempest, the Spitfire Mk XII and XIV and, ultimately, the Gloster Meteor. However, its credentials as an effective weapon of war could not be faulted, as the roll call of its battle honours on the banner to the right of the rostrum clearly showed. Indeed, whilst the entire workforce at the Langley plant enjoyed their break from the assembly line, and senior representatives from Hawkers, the Air Ministry and the RAF congratulated each other on the type's astounding combat history, over a dozen units were at that very moment continuing to add to its list of battle honours in the Far East, the Balkans and along the D-Day front. This shot was taken by Hawkers at the aircraft's official handing-over ceremony to the RAF on 15 September 1944 *(via Aeroplane)*

check the position of the fuel selector cock, which could be set to reserve or main tanks – later in the war further controls for external tanks were added. On start up you would always use the gravity-fed reserve supply, reselecting to the external tanks, or main, once safely airborne. With the stick uncomfortably held fully aft in the pilot's stomach, the throttle was opened about an inch, taking into account the backlash felt through the left hand. Once the engine fired up you would open the throttle a little more, then gently ease it back to warm up rpm.

'The pitch lever controlling the angle of attack of the propeller blades had to be in the forward position. Once this final check had been carried out, you signalled thumbs up to your groundcrew, who would then whisk the chocks away. To avoid the aeroplane immediately nosing over once the throttle was blipped, the pilot had to ensure that the control column was kept pulled firmly back. We had this point so drummed home to us by our instructors that one thought that it was almost a court-martial offence not to cuddle one's control column full aft!

'Starting up the Rolls-Royce Merlin itself involved unscrewing the ubiquitous Ki-Gass pump, pushing its plunger in and out, and thus passing neat fuel into the powerplant. One-and-a-half to two pumps of the Ki-Gass was usually adequate to coax the Merlin into life, depending on the weather temperature, and one would keep the device open just in case more neat fuel was needed until the engine ran smoothly. Most aeroplanes of this era had a Ki-Gass fitted, and it really didn't feel normal if you jumped into a machine that lacked one! With the fuel flowing and ignition switches on, you simultaneously pressed the starter-motor and booster coil buttons – actions which were soon followed by a marvellous crackle from the engine as it barked into life.

'As you gained experience on the Hurricane you evolved techniques to encourage a smooth engine start-up every time. Occasionally on start up the propeller would try to kick back, as if it wanted to go the other way. In order to eradicate this rather worrying trait, some of us used an unorthodox starting procedure which you wouldn't find in any pilot's notes on the Hurricane. I would activate the booster coil and the starter button with the ignition switches off, then flick the latter on as the engine began to fire. With the engine running, the first thing you would do was to check the oil pressure gauge to ensure that it was registering correctly. The Ki-Gass was then screwed back down into the closed position.

'Satisfied that the Merlin was behaving itself, you would then check that the brake pressures were okay, the temperature and pressure gauges were indicating correctly and finally ensure that the engine-driven hydraulic pump was operating successfully by deploying and retracting the flaps again. The position of the latter was indicated by a flap gauge, which consisted of a mechanical pointer mounted within the cockpit in a position not readily visible to the pilot. I therefore took to feeling the pointer in later years, rather than just looking at it, so as to be sure that when I put the flaps down and then selected them up, they had indeed gone fully up.

'As you taxied away from dispersal you would adopt a weaving pattern from side to side in order to gain a modest level of visibility over the nose, thus reducing the chances of a collision – taxying mishaps were one of the most frowned upon of all misdemeanours that a young "Bog Rat" pilot could involve himself with. Whilst gingerly taxying you kept a watchful eye on the brake pressure by monitoring a three-needled gauge which indicated main air pressure supply and the pressures on each under-carriage wheel. You also quickly developed a feel for the brakes.

'Once lined up on the runway, you opened the throttle to a sensible rpm, whilst all the time keeping the stick pulled fully back into your stomach – a position you maintained from the moment the engine kicked into life, even though it was a slightly awkward thing to have to do. As you slowly continued to pour on the power you relaxed the stick to the neutral position and the aircraft rolled down the runway. At the same time you initially fed on up to full starboard rudder to keep the aircraft straight. If you pushed the throttle wide open from the start the aeroplane would swing uncontrollably to port. However, as you became familiar with it you could unleash a tremendous amount of power early on, just as long as you anticipated the Hurricane's directional handling characteristics and duly compensated for them. Care was also necessary when easing the stick forward to raise the tail to ensure that the propeller did not hit the ground.

'One kept on a straight take-off path by using peripheral vision out of either side of the cockpit, checking your position against the edges of the runway, or, when on grass, in relation to other objects you would have focused on as you sat waiting for clearance to take-off. The nose of the aircraft was then allowed to rise gently, but if you rotated prematurely at a lower airspeed you would find the Hurricane a little bit left wing low as a result of the engine torque and the offset thrust. Seconds after becoming airborne you swapped hands on the control column and selected gear up, then quickly returned to the traditional left hand on the throttle and right hand on the stick arrangement.

'The engine was now happily growling away at 3000 rpm, with the boost level varying depending on the standard of engine fitted to the Hurricane and the technique you had adopted for take-off – the latter could see you limiting the boost level and not using full throttle in order to save wear and tear on the engine when you took off. Climbing speed to operational height was usually around 135 mph, and whilst gaining altitude you would be constantly correcting the aeroplane directionally. The key to precision airmanship was to fly symmetrically, and to achieve this you had to keep the slip needle in the middle of the dial at all times. This became crucial

Right The Last of the Many! enjoyed a brief period of celebrity status in the violent summer of 1944, being paraded through Kingston following its roll out. Soon after this event it returned to Langley, where it was flown like any other Hawker product by the company's Chief Test Pilot, P W S 'George' Bulman, who had now been promoted to the rank of Group Captain. After passing all the stipulated checks laid down by the Ministry of Aircraft Production, the Hurricane was deemed ready for acceptance by the RAF. This evocative shot of a barely used PZ865 was taken by Hawker's legendary photographer, Cyril Peckham, between the aircraft's first flight date and its handing over to the air force – the photographer used Hawker's Hart as a camera-ship on this sortie. Sitting comfortably within the heavily framed cockpit of the machine, Bulman appears to have dispensed with headgear altogether for this flight (he wore just a trilby back in November 1935 for the first flight of K5083!), obviously preferring to communicate with the photographer by hand signals. The four Oerlikon 20 mm cannon, whose barrels protrude prominently from the wing leading edge, were fitted to the fighter for a very brief time only *(via Aeroplane)*

later on when it came to firing the guns because if your aircraft slipped or skidded through the air, you would never hit your target.

'To keep the Hurricane in a symmetrical state you had to adjust the rudder trim frequently, a fact you soon got used to in most propeller-driven aeroplanes if you wanted to fly them professionally.

'On these early flights from Hullavington I would climb to a sensible altitude and just cruise around at about 250 to 300 mph, checking the effect of the lateral control and the rate at which you could bank the aeroplane to the left or right. The ease and accuracy with which you could maintain height in maximum rate turns was critically investigated. The directional trim required constant correction to centre the slip needle. You soon found out that as you increased speed the lateral control became heavier and heavier until it was impossible to manoeuvre at high speed. I found that the best speed for lateral control in the Hurricane was 200 to 250 mph.

Above By late 1944 the RAF had more than enough Hurricane IIcs to see it through to war's end, so PZ865 was bailed back to Hawkers for its communications flight. In December 1945 it was bought outright by the company for private use and placed in storage. Mothballed for almost five years, the fighter was finally given a new lease of life in the spring of 1950 when it was entered by Princess Margaret in that year's King's Cup Race. Fully overhauled and civilianised by Hawkers to meet ARB requirements, it emerged with a whip aerial in place of its traditional mast, two extra 12.5 gal fuel tanks and minus its distinctive wing cannon and fairings – interestingly enough, four Oerlikons have always been available to fit back into the wings of PZ865, but a set of the associated barrel fairings have never been traced! It was resprayed royal blue and gold and issued with the registration G-AMAU. It made its public debut, with Hawkers then Chief Test Pilot 'Wimpy' Wade at the controls, at the Royal Aeronautical Society's Garden Party at White Waltham on 14 May 1950 – the day after its first flight in restored form. Issued with a special Certificate of Airworthiness that cleared it solely for air racing, record breaking and demonstration flights, it was flown to second place in the King's Cup Race by Grp Capt Peter Townsend at an average speed of 283 mph on 17 June that same year. This dramatic *Flight* photograph was snapped during the event, and it shows Battle of Britain veteran Townsend banking tightly around one of the beacons out on the course, revealing the aircraft's race number in the process (*via Aeroplane*)

'The aeroplane was very appealing to a novice pilot particularly when it came to recovering back to the airfield after flying serenely over Wiltshire. The wide-track undercarriage, with its very fat and soft low-pressure tyres, made the Hurricane ideal for operations from unprepared areas. It was a friendly aircraft, and could be abused with little fear of it biting back – hence the fact that even a sprog like Bedford could handle it back in those formative flying days of 1941. Years later the Hunter exhibited those same friendly characteristics, and was described by as "a real pilot's aeroplane".

'Looking back, the only real criticisms I had of the Hurricane from a novice pilot's point of view centred around the heavy lateral forces transmitted through the stick at high speeds. In achieving the latter, the aircraft suffered its second fault – engine cut out when applying negative-g. This problem also afflicted the Spitfire of course, and meant that when you pushed the nose down into a dive, there was an abrupt misfire as the Merlin was starved of fuel and your acceleration was impeded accordingly. Therefore, if you were trying to get away from something you would slow down in the first instance if you pushed the stick forward! This problem was a service operational limitation on the engine, and thus on the aircraft, and necessitated a rolling entry into a slightly delayed dive.

'The Hurricane's main protagonist in 1940, the Bf 109E, was powered by a Daimler-Benz engine (the DB 601) which used fuel injection, and thus did not suffer the hiccups of the Merlin when pushed into a dive. An ingenious interim solution to the Merlin's gravity-fed SU float-chamber carburettors was provided by a clever lady engineer from the Royal Aircraft Establishment Farnborough named Miss Shilling. She designed a small metal diaphragm with a hole in the middle that was fitted into the float chamber, thus ensuring that even under negative-g, there was sufficient fuel flow to feed the engine. This brilliantly simple device was quickly christened "Miss Shilling's orifice".

'As one progressed on the course a brief phase of aerobatics was performed, although no spinning was permitted at this early stage. Postwar, I carried out considerable erect spinning trials with Hawker's own Hurricane. I found that it wound up quite well and took a number of turns to recover from the spin. To achieve a spin you pulled the stick hard back and applied full rudder and away it went, and when it came time to recover you pushed the stick fully forward and applied full opposite rudder. It was quite straight forward to recover from the spin, although as the number of turns increased it became more reluctant to recover without first requiring full rudder for some considerable period of time.

'I learnt to aerobat the Hurricane looping at 230 to 250 mph and rolling at 200 to 220 mph. It really had a good power-to-weight ratio for its time, and it "went around corners" very well. I personally think that it had a better turn rate than the Spitfire, but pilots of the latter fighter may disagree!

'When comparing the two great RAF fighters of 1940, it is worth bearing in mind that the Hurricane's simple structure saw it built in two-thirds of the man-hours it took to manufacture a Spitfire. Of course the latter was truly loved because of its marvellous name, faster speed and exquisite lines, whereas the Hurricane was humpier and plumper, and enjoyed far more modest publicity. The Hawker fighter was a workhorse whilst the Spitfire was an altogether more highly-bred device that required more attention to both manufacture and to fly. Its undercarriage wasn't entirely suited to rough fields, and its handling less forgiving of novice pilots.

'Towards the end of your conversion you would practice gunnery work using ciné film on drogue target passes. It was possible to give a false impression when using the ciné camera by skidding onto the target on your firing passes to achieve passable marks, but the folly of this was starkly exposed out in Burma by our OC at No 267 Wing, the legendary Wg Cdr Frank "Chotah" Carey. A brilliant Hurricane pilot of boundless modesty and slight stature, he would say, "Gentleman. There are four main elements of air combat – range, line, deflection and good flying. You can cheat when you are using a ciné camera, but remember that when the chips are down and you do it operationally, if you have become accustomed to flying slovenly with skid on, you will probably get shot down instead of your opponent." Few could argue with him due to his impressive war record of 26 kills confirmed and seven probables!

'Upon leaving Hullavington with 13 hours and 35 minutes Hurricane flying under my belt I was sent literally up the road to Aston Down and No 52 Operational Training Unit. Here, I gained experience on radio homing, formation flying, ground firing, radio procedure practice, navigation on cross-country flights, cloud flying, forced-landing practice, aerobatics and some spinning and air combat. I eventually finished there with 46 hours on the Hurricane. Upon my graduation in August 1941 I was sent to RAF Honiley, just south of Coventry, to No 605 "County of Warwickshire" Sqn on Hurricane IIcs, with whom I stayed for just a short while. Here, I performed sector reconnaissance, anti-aircraft co-operation, which saw us beating up gun posts, and myriad other tasks – so much so that I logged 28 hours in the cockpit during my first month with the squadron, which was a mix of low and high level flying, with particular emphasis on close formation and loose battle formation flying.

No 605 Sqn was then given its marching orders to head out to the beleaguered island of Malta, which it duly did, but due to my lack of experience it was deemed prudent to transfer me to fellow-Honiley residents No 135 Sqn, where I was accepted in October 1941. Here, I was exposed for the first time to long-range flying in the Hurricane, and in those days the aircraft was configured for this type of sortie by simply bolting two fixed drop tanks under the wings.

Above G-AMAU's smart factory racing scheme was subtly modified on several occasions during the first half of the 1950s, the three gold cheat lines down the side of its fuselage, for instance, being applied in varying lengths for different races. Aside from Peter Townsend's admirable second place in the fighter's debut event in June 1950, G-AMAU also finished third at the Kemsley Trophy Race at Swansea (with Neville Duke at the controls) two months later, before capping the season off in September by setting the fastest time in the Daily Express Challenge Trophy Race. For these later events Hawker's engineers had re-engined PZ865 with a Merlin 24, thus allowing it to match the speeds of its great rival, the privately-owned Spitire Vb AB910 *(British Aerospace via Mike Stroud)*

'The technique adopted for flying the aircraft with these ungauged, and "draggy", items under the wings was as follows – you would never have seen this procedure recommended in pilot's notes! You operated a star-shaped control on the right hand side of the console which opened the valve for your starboard tank, then with fingers crossed you turned off the main fuel supply cock and looked at your watch, for you knew that for a predetermined time you could fly on the contents of this external store. A small red fuel light was fitted on the instrument panel to warn you when the tank was empty, but because the sun shining into the cockpit often negated the effects of the light's illumination, usually the first thing you knew about the tank being empty was when the engine gave an all mighty hiccup, spluttered and eventually stopped.

'You would then leap into action by throttling back the engine and switching on and priming fuel up from the reserve tank. After breathing a sigh of relief at having caught the Merlin before it cut out completely, you would then proceed to tidy up the cockpit by shutting off the "star wheel" on the right and turning on its opposite number on the left hand side of the cockpit. Then, with some trepidation, the main fuel cock was shut off once again and another little timed expedition commenced, but this time by courtesy of the port tank! These tanks made the aeroplane far less manoeuvrable, as "Chotah" Carey reinforced to us "sprog" pilots immediately upon our arrival in Burma. "There's not a cat in Hell's chance of any of you turning with the Japanese Army Ki 97 "Nates". They aren't flown by pilots with thick spectacles, who are inexperienced and have lousy aeroplanes. They can kill you like anything else. There is only one way to attack them, and that is by going in fast from up sun and getting the hell out of it after you've made your pass. Don't try and turn with them because you won't be able to, and you'll end up getting shot down."

'No 135 Sqn also received its marching orders soon after I arrived, and by the beginning of December I found myself aboard the SS *Durban Castle*, heading for parts unknown, which duly turned out to be the Far East. We were put ashore on the West African coast and flown by Lodestar across to Cairo. There, our senior pilots immediately wangled four or five Hurricanes and flew on to Burma in stages to tackle the invading Japanese, whilst the rest of us sat around for a while awaiting the next delivery of crated Hurricanes to arrive from Britain.

'Eventually, we got away in groups of six Hurricane IIbs, with a single Blenheim escort, from Cairo and routed through Iraq and India in short, easy, stages until we finally arrived at Mingaladon on 11 February 1942, just in time to fly a handful of escort sorties for Blenheims and Lysanders, who were attempting to stem the flow of Japanese troops swarming westward through Burma. The mix of a formation of Lysanders equipped with two 250 lb bombs and Hurricane escorts hamstrung by fixed underwing drop tanks, unsurprisingly failed to seriously dent the morale of the enemy and we duly evacuated Mingaladon only days after my arrival – due to a shortage of Hurricanes I headed west by boat until eventually arriving at Dum Dum, Calcutta. However, a handful of remaining squadron pilots gave a good account of themselves in the face of a far bigger enemy force, several not living to tell the tale.

For the next eight months I performed various exercises with the squadron including sector reconnaissance, beam attacks, ferrying new aircraft from Karachi, convoy patrols and air to ground strafing work. Periodically we would be scrambled to intercept enemy recce aircraft supposedly sighted in our vicinity but we never saw anything. The squadron had to regularly disperse to forward sites nicknamed "Dung Cow", "Dirty Dick" and "Dunster". I performed a considerable number of routine post-inspection air tests simply because I enjoyed flying. This continual routine came to an abrupt halt on Christmas Day 1942 when, as a passenger, I was almost killed in a Chevrolet station wagon heading out to dispersal at dawn after one of our pilots rolled the vehicle. Sgt Plt Ford was killed instantly, and I teetered on the brink of death for two weeks, having suffered a fractured pelvis and back, plus a ruptured kidney.

Fortunately I made a full recovery, but I didn't fly for nine months. Meanwhile, No 135 Sqn went back into Burma and achieved considerable success, but not without the loss of a number of pilots. Perhaps fate decreed that the near thing in the car meant I avoided curtains in Burma!

Right Aside from participating in a variety of other events ranging from the Kemsley Trophy Race at Swansea to the Daily Express Challenge Trophy Race, G-AMAU temporarily donned wartime markings for a brief appearance alongside several Portuguese Hurricanes in the classic 1950 war film *Angels One Five*. In 1956 it was transferred to Dunsfold airfield and later repainted in its 1944 delivery scheme. By the late 1950s one pilot was becoming synonymous with its operation – Hawker's Chief Test Pilot, Bill Bedford. Well qualified to fly the veteran machine, Bedford had seen combat in Hurricane IIb/cs and over the jungles of Burma in 1942/43, and had well over 600 hours on the type by the time he joined the company soon after the war. Many interesting details like the extended foot stirrup and opened hand-hold (activated by deploying the stirrup) are visible in this wonderful PR shot, as is the canopy sliding handle. To the left of the pilot's hand is a small zap that looks remarkably like the No 23 Sqn eagle *(British Aerospace via Bill Bedford)*

Left Bill Bedford's displays in Hawker aircraft are the stuff of legend, and although he is best remembered for spirited performances in the Hunter T.7 and P.1127 at prestigious venues like Farnborough and Le Bourget, he was equally at home flying low-level 'beat ups' for small groups of Air Training Corps (ATC) cadets, as this stunning shot shows. Flying up the slope of the Hog's Back in Surrey, Bedford was putting PZ865 through its paces in a private display staged specially for his son's ATC squadron in the mid-1960s. Seconds away from cracking their heads on the roof of their car, the occupants of the Vauxhall Viva in the foreground seem totally oblivious to the rapidly closing *Last of the Many!* – they should have checked their mirrors *(via Bill Bedford)*

HAWKER'S HURRICANE

'By the time I left the RAF to join Hawkers as experimental test pilot I had completed 485 hours on the Hurricane between June 1941 and May 1944, with only my period in plaster having kept me off operational flying. Prior to leaving the air force I had attended a course at the Empire Test Pilots' School both as a student and a tutor, and was soon after approached by Hawkers, who were looking for an experimental test pilot. Sqn Ldr Trevor "Wimpy" Wade had been killed in the crash of the prototype Hawker P.1081 on 3 April 1951, and my revered friend Neville Duke had taken over as Chief Test Pilot, with me as his No 2. We flew all manner of fine Hawker designs ranging from the Sea Fury through to the Hunter. After a brilliant career with Hawkers, Neville retired with an injured back following several nasty crashes, and I took over as Chief Test Pilot in 1956, with Hugh Merewether as my No 2. Shortly after taking over this position, interest in V/STOL aircraft grew and I was involved with pioneer experimental flying on Hawker's P.1127, Kestrel and Harrier, performing the first flights on each.

'The bonus to all this exhilarating flying was the fact that Hawkers operated a vintage fleet of aircraft which included the 1924 Cygnet, the Hart, the Tomtit, a Whitney Straight, an Avro Anson a D H Rapide and the Hurricane. I joined the company in September 1951, and flew the Hurricane from Shoreham back to the factory airfield at Langley a matter

Above A slightly larger crowd witnessed this display of precision flying by Hawker's Chief Test Pilot at the RAF Wattisham Battle of Britain Day in September 1967. Retracing his steps at 15 ft and 250 kts, Bedford powers down the live flightline between rows of Shackletons and Lightnings. Always a stickler for safety in the display arena, he had earlier walked down the ramp checking that separation distances between the two lines of aircraft allowed him to perform the pass with adequate space on either wingtip. He later summed up the display in the following sentence; 'Do as I say, don't do as I do!' *(Peter M Warren via Bill Bedford)*

of days after my arrival – it had performed at an airshow at the Sussex field the previous weekend. To show how much aircraft had improved in the intervening decade since I had learnt to fly the Hurricane, I now viewed this machine as a wonderful piece of vintage kit to fly when compared with all the new jet types we were then involved with on a daily basis. I was no longer in awe of it, although I treated it with the utmost respect.

However, as I began to fly it more regularly at airshows in the summer months and on visits to various RAF stations on business, it began to establish a warm feeling within me. In the early 1950s I established something of a double act with the legendary Jeffery Quill who was flying Spitfire AB910 at selected Battle of Britain air days. We were in constant demand in the summer, and to ease our task, Jeffery would occupy one sector of the airfield and I would simply perform my manoeuvres adjacent to him, but with safe lateral separation. We thus flew "co-ordinated aerobatics" to the unbridled delight of the crowd. Occasionally we would perform gentle dogfights as well, the fame of our aircraft seeing us booked at shows as far apart as Leuchars, in Scotland, to the Channel Islands. I would often return to Dunsfold at first light on a Monday morning, revelling in the emptiness of the sky and enjoying every moment in the cockpit of PZ865. It really became a faithful friend, and never let me down.

Indeed, I felt so close to the Hurricane that I was given sideways glances for clocking up so many hours in it. I think PZ865 expected to be flown by me because I had developed a special affection for it! It really was a privilege to be able to fly such a historic machine, and be able to use it to visit both the Fleet Air Arm Sea Hawk and RAF Hunter bases. These were the halcyon days of aviation as you could fly up to eight or nine different types a month as par for the course.

'Almost 30 years on, I look at the Hurricane and see an aeroplane I could quite happily strap myself straight back into and fly safely once again, although perhaps without quite the same degree of refinement as of yore!'

Left A great companion for Bill Bedford and Hawker's Hurricane between 1955 and 1962 was Jeffrey Quill in Vickers-Armstrongs' Spitfire Vb AB910. A war veteran with confirmed combat kills, this machine had also been air raced in the King's Cup of 1950 in private hands. Damaged in a landing accident soon after, it was repaired by Vickers-Armstrongs, who then decided to buy it in 1955. Upon being restored to airworthiness it was repainted in No 92 Sqn colours, primarily because the unit's code letters partly matched the initials of the company's then Chief Test Pilot, Jeffrey Quill. An unofficial partnership was soon forged between the two great test pilots, and the Spitfire and Hurricane were much in demand across the UK. This evocative shot was taken towards the end their 'special relationship' in mid-1965, AB910 being presented back to the RAF's Historic Flight in September of that year. Quill's last flight in a Spitfire was made in this machine specifically for a French TV documentary in the spring of 1966 at RAF Coltishall, then home of the Historic Flight *(British Aerospace via Bill Bedford)*

Above Many famous dignitaries had their photographs taken with *Last of the Many!* whilst it was in Hawker's hands, one of whom was the then Australian Prime Minister, Sir John Gorton. A conservative who followed Sir Robert Menzies into power in the late 1960s, Sir John had more reason than most to pause for a moment's reflection while in the cockpit of the aircraft – he had flown Hurricane IIbs in defence of Singapore with No 242(I) Sqn in February 1942, being shot up and having to force-land on one occasion. During the controlled crash Gorton was flung forward in his straps and smashed his nose on the gunsight, hence his boxer-like profile. Ironically, considering the aircraft's Bill Bedford connection, the future Australian Prime Minister had also served briefly with No 135 Sqn prior to joining the ranks of the composite No 242 on the embattled island *(British Aerospace via Bill Bedford)*

Left This remarkable shot was taken in 1966 as a tribute to the genius of Sir Sydney Camm, the aircraft being arranged at Dunsfold in the shape of a 'C'. Running in an anti-clockwise direction, the formation consists of a Cygnet, Hart, Tomtit, Hurricane IIc, engineless Sea Fury, Sea Hawk, Hunter F.6, Hunter F.7 and Harrier GR.1 *(British Aerospace via Bill Bedford)*

Above Part of the unofficial Hawker Museum, the Hurricane was re-engined with a Merlin 502 in 1962, which allowed it to continue its routine of regular airshow appearances. In 1967 it became 'H3424' for the *Battle of Britain* film, wearing the spurious codes 'MI-G' and 'KV-M' on different occasions. When this shot was taken on a damp spring day at A & AEE Boscombe Down, in Hampshire, in 1971, G-AMAU was just entering its final year in Hawker Siddeley's hands as it was presented to the Battle of Britain Memorial Flight (BBMF) exactly 12 months later *(Jeremy Flack)*

Left 'Somewhere in a field in southern England . . .' Ready for a quick reaction scramble at Dunsfold aerodrome, Bill Bedford hams it up for the chief photographer of the Surrey Advertiser in 1966. The heavy usage made of PZ865 by Hawker's Chief Test Pilot is clearly visible in this elevated view, the chipped prop boss and weathered leading edges of the Dowty propeller blades denoting that the veteran fighter did indeed earn its keep during the 1950s and 60s *(K Rimell via Bill Bedford)*

Above Soon after it was delivered to the Flight's then Coltishall base, PZ865 was stripped of its late war camouflage and repainted in the famous December 1940 scheme of Hurricane Mk I V6962, flown by the then Sqn Ldr Robert Stanford-Tuck's, OC of No 257 'Burma' Sqn, whilst stationed at North Weald. His machine was unusual because it retained the half-black/half-duck egg blue underside camouflage so favoured by Fighter Command in the early months of the war, but soon discarded as being all but useless by most units by August 1940 due to its ineffectiveness in the combat environment, as Pete Brothers (who was a flight commander under Stanford-Tuck at No 257 at the time) explains. 'The upper surface camouflage worked well over land, whereas the German fighters with their greys and brightly coloured noses stood out prominently from some distance. Of course we had the curious half-black/half-duck egg blue underside scheme in the early days of the conflict, thus denoting our night- and dayfighter roles. This really was a quite ridiculous idea!' Seen here sharing a ramp at RAF Upper Heyford in August 1972 with Belgian Air Force F-104s and Noratlas transports, PZ865 wears totally authentic markings for 'DT-A', except for the dayglo 'kill' added after the row of Swastikas – this denotes a birdstrike experienced in the machine by a Flight pilot only a matter of weeks before this shot was taken. A second birdstrike occurred in 1975 *(Jeremy Flack)*

Above PZ865 spent much of the 1970s in its No 257 Sqn colours, sharing the airshow duties with the Flight's other Hurricane IIc, LF363. Airworthy for most of the decade, it did, howver, spend a period of 12 months grounded between September 1975 and August 1976 whilst awaiting the arrival of a new radiator to replace the corroded original which had been installed at Langley in 1944. Whilst grounded the BBMF took the opportunity to repaint the airframe in its delivery scheme as a tribute to those who built the fighter during the war, as well as to mark the 50th anniversary of K5083's first flight. PZ865 flew for a short spell in the mid-1980s painted up as 'JU-Q' of No 111 Sqn, but in early 1986 was resprayed in the scheme so associated with the airframe, and featured in this moody head-on shot taken near Coningsby in the spring of that year *(Richard Winslade)*

Left Arguably the most important pair of aircraft within the BBMF's highly valued fleet, PZ865 is joined by Spitfire IIa P7530 at medium altitude over Kent during a return flight from Manston to Coningsby on 30 September 1982. Unlike the former, which was never really part of the RAF proper, P7530 served with four squadrons within Fighter Command during its 12 months at the 'sharp end' between August 1940 and August 1941 – Nos 266, 603, 616 and 64 Sqns, in order of assignment *(Richard Winslade)*

Above and right Wg Cdr John Ward tucks PZ865 in behind the photographer's Lancaster camera-ship before diving away below the big bomber's left wing. The Hurricane is heavy in all axes when flown during a typical display, bleeding off speed rapidly and in turn taking longer to regain it than the Spitfire. When describing the fighter's general handling characteristics whilst performing modest aerobatics, Wg Cdr Ward once wrote that, 'the Hurricane will go round a display like its Spitfire counterpart, but requires extensive and constant use of elevator trim to lighten the load, and extensive use of rudder in conjunction with aileron to produce a respective rate of roll. It is thus vital that rolling manoeuvres are commenced with a respectably high nose-up attitude to counter the slow roll-rate and avoid excitement' *(Richard Winslade)*

Above Looking somewhat lost in amongst the Hardened Aircraft Shelters
(HAS) at RAF Alconbury during the base open day in 1986, PZ865 awaits its
turn to perform in front of the huge crowd. Due to its tiring flying
characteristics when put through its paces, crews have evolved a smooth and
loose routine over the years at the BBMF, avoiding the tight point-display
performances favoured by civilian pilots in Mustangs and late-marque
Spitfires. Dwarfed by the gaping HAS behind the Hurricane is a privately-
owned F4U Corsair *(Jeremy Flack)*

Above Far more at home on the lush grass outside the BBMF's period T2 hangar at Coningsby, PZ865 sits alongside LF363 with its straps splayed over the edge of the cockpit, awaiting the word to 'scramble' at the base open day in 1986. Aside from the markedly different camouflage schemes, the two Hurricanes were near identical in spec, a factor which eased both type conversion for novice pilots assigned to the Flight, and the training of engineers tasked with keeping the Hawker fighters airborne (*Jeremy Flack*)

Left A slogan that will always be associated with PZ865, *Last of the Many!* was applied to the fixed panel beneath the cockpit on both sides of the aircraft weeks before the rest of the machine was fabricated and sprayed in the factory camouflage of the period. This sobriquet was a jocular reply by Hawkers to the title of the 1942 film about the life of the late R J Mitchell, entitled *The First of the Few (Richard Winslade)*

Above Seemingly sheltering from the elements at a cold and blustery Duxford in 1987, PZ865 sits chocked in front of the BBMF's flagship, Lancaster B.I PA474. Limited to only 100 hours flying annually, the Hurricane is much in demand across the UK due to it being the only one of its type within the Flight. In order to keep it in as sound a condition as possible, the fighter is barely wound up to speeds in excess of 207 mph, and when cruising at its preferred 172 mph, it burns 40 Imp gal per hour *(John Dibbs)*

Left If a Merlin fails to turn over once power is run through from the 12-volt trolley acc, nine times out of ten it means that the magneto is playing up. It may have got dirty during the previous ignition, or be suffering from damp in cold weather. In either case the remedy is much the same as it was over 50 years ago – whip the engine cowling off and turn the problem over to the nearest fitter! This little problem was soon nutted out on the Coningsby ramp in late summer 1992, and PZ865 sent aloft for a post rectification check flight. Note the dayglo 'splayed duck' symbol below the cockpit, denoting yet another birdstrike survived *(Mike Vines)*

Above Having finally got the magneto problem sorted, the Hurricane performed its short test flight in the Coningsby locale, with Sqn Ldr Paul Day at the controls. Once back on the ground, the pilot wandered off into the crewroom to fill out his post-sortie notes on the machine's behaviour, whilst the groundcrew shackled the fighter up to their less than period tow tractor and pulled it back into the hangar for inspection. Parked behind the Hurricane are two of the Flight's Spitfires, namely PS853 (one of two Mk XIXs then with the BBMF) and P7350 (the Mk IIa) *(Mike Vines)*

Above Although the size (and, accordingly, price) of the equipment may have changed over the intervening 50 years, the procedure for refuelling a Hurricane has hardly altered. The basic Hawker fighter has three tanks fitted to it – one in each wing inboard of the guns, and a single tank immediately forward of the cockpit. These combined to give the fighter a range of approximately 500 miles at a cruising speed of 176 mph. PZ865, however, boasts a further two wing tanks (12 gal capacity each) which were fitted by Hawkers back in 1950 in place of the cannon. When fully fuelled up, this machine is severely restricted in its manoeuvrability, so pilots are thoroughly instructed at an early stage in their type conversion on maximum fuel weights permissible for the commencement of aerobatics. Ironically, only these extra tanks are fitted with a low-level warning system, the remaining three cells having their contents measured by the amount of time the engine has been fuelled by them! Finally, tank selection is an entirely manual affair, so it soon becomes obvious to pilots new to the Flight why one of the more important lessons taught to themduring the conversion course on to the Hurricane is effective fuel management *(Mike Vines)*

Right A dedicated cadre of 21 full-time engineers are on strength with the BBMF at any one time throughout the year, tradesmen and women seeing a posting to the unit as being a quick way to achieve total job satisfaction within the air force. The Flight conducts continual 'on the job' training for its new recruits, which usually lasts between six to nine months, and after which they are considered competent to work with minimal supervision. A vast library of Air Ministry publications and manufacturers' drawings and repair manuals are held by the Flight, thus ensuring that a sound technical archive is always available to the engineering team. Each aircraft also has a full service log stretching back to its first flight, and from these major overhaul dates for individual machines are scheduled. The Hurricane received a major servicing every 180 hours during wartime, but 50 years on, PZ865 only has a 'major' every 360 hours, or six years. This is primarily because the airframe is carefully looked after at Coningsby, with intermediate checks being carried out either annually, or every 60 hours. As part of this programme of continual 'TLC', two groundcrewmen go about checking the hydraulic oxygen pressure line attached to the port oleo of PZ865 *(Richard Winslade)*

Above The end result of the many long hours working in the draughty hangar at Coningsby are seen in this close up and personal view of PZ865, with Wg Cdr David Moss at the controls, taken in mid-1992. The distinctive cowling fairing blisters are clearly visible in this shot, as are the unique splayed engine ejector stubs associated with the Merlin 502. When the machine was originally built in 1944 it was fitted with a standard Merlin XX (as installed in all Mk IIcs), which had a three-stub exhaust arrangement, but following its first re-engining in August 1950 with a Merlin 24, the stubs were replaced with a six-ejector layout similar to that fitted to late marque Spitfires. In 1962 a Merlin 502 was installed, and yet another style of exhaust stubs appeared on the fighter. Today, the splayed ejectors seen in this shot seem to be the most common type used by PZ865, although the more historically accurate three-stub exhausts were utilised by the Flight on the aircraft for a very brief period in 1986 *(John Dibbs)*

Right With the engine burbling along and the wind whipping in to the open cockpit, Wg Cdr Moss would be hard pressed to hear anything over the intercom. Indeed, whilst performing an aerobatics routine, the pilot has to throttle back if he wants to communicate effectively over the R/T as the din in the cockpit with the engine on display power settings is totally deafening. Back in 1939, the idea of fighters with enclosed cockpits was a relatively new one, the immortal Gloster Gladiator being the first in-service type to boast such an arrangement. For the many Gauntlet pilots who went straight from biplanes to monoplanes in the form of the Spitfire or Hurricane, this new experience was a most pleasurable one (despite the engine noise), as Pete Brothers explained to the author. 'The Hurricanes made a wonderful change from our old Gauntlet biplanes. Now, instead of having your head battered by the slipstream in the open cockpit of the Gloster fighter, the Hurricane was nice and cosy, with the canopy over the top' *(John Dibbs)*

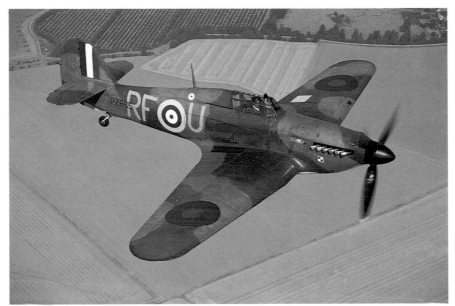

Left After a long period in plain 1944 Fighter Command colours, PZ865 was resprayed by the Flight in 1989 to mark the 50th anniversary celebrations for the Battle of Britain that were scheduled for the following year. Many different schemes were contemplated, but finally a decision was made to finish the aircraft in the colours of a Hurricane Mk I of No 303 'Warsaw-Kosciuszko' Sqn, the highest scoring unit of the Battle of Britain with 117.5 victories. Of the many machines used by the Polish squadron during the summer of 1940 – 58 in total – one Hurricane stood out as being the most significant – P3975, serial 'RF-U'. This machine was the favoured mount of the leading pilot of the Battle, Czech-born Sgt Josef Frantisek, who claimed 17 kills during the month of September 1940. In fact, he scored his first victory in P3975 on 2 September, a 9./JG 51 Bf 109E-1 that crashed in the Channel. Another Messerschmitt fell to his guns the following day, and then both a Bf 109E and an He 111 were downed by Frantisek in P3975 six days later. However, on this latter sortie the Czech was forced to land near Brighton after running out of fuel, damaging his much-loved Hurricane in the process. It played no further part in the Battle, and Frantisek was later killed on 8 October in R4175 'R-FR' when his fighter inexplicably crashed whilst on patrol over Surrey *(John Dibbs)*

Above By the time this shot of PZ865 was taken from the BBMF's Devon hack in mid-1992, 'RF-U' was beginning to look a lot more like an authentic Battle of Britain aircraft in terms of its paint finish than it had done two years previously The olive drab and earth shades had weathered nicely over the intervening period, and patches of airframe primer were beginning to peak through immediately aft of the exhaust stubs. Fluid and fuel stains were smeared all over the forward fuselage, and only the pristine nature of the roundels and code letters made PZ865 look any different from P3975 of 52 years before *(John Dibbs)*

In early September 1990 most RAF squadrons were busy brushing up their formation flying for the massed flypast over London that marked the 50th anniversary of the Battle of Britain. Forming the focal point for the 150-aircraft spectacle, the BBMF had to make sure that their own formation work was up to scratch, and as these previously unpublished shots show, it certainly was. Photographed from a Hawk during a practice sortie over Lincolnshire, all eight of the Flight's aircraft were sent aloft to ensure that pilots got used to separation distances and general station keeping for long periods of time *(British Aerospace/Geoff Lee via Mike Stroud)*

Right Throughout a typical airshow season from May through to October, the BBMF will attend over 60 events ranging in size from the International Air Tattoo and Farnborough through to small village fetes overflown en route to bigger shows. The Flight like to try and display the Hurricane at as many of these events as possible, which often means that PZ865 shares the fighter slots with any one of the four Spitfires currently operated from Coningsby. This shot, taken in mid-1989, shows the Hurricane being escorted during the course of its weekend's work by Spitfire Mk Vb AB910, which wears the markings of a presentation aircraft flown by No 457 'Australian' Sqn from the Isle of Man in mid-1941. This scheme was applied to the fighter just prior to the 50th anniversary of the Spitfire's first flight, which was celebrated on 5 March 1986. The inscription 'In Memory of R. J. Mitchell' was worn on X4936 of No 457 Sqn, having been sponsored in its construction by Mr Fred Pearson, the director of the American Clinic in Vienna which nursed R J Mitchell just prior to his death on 11 June 1937. AB910 retained this scheme up until 1990, thus honouring the Spitfire's designer throughout the 50th anniversary year of his death *(Richard Winslade)*

Above Over the years almost two-dozen different schemes and codes have been worn by the Hurricanes and Spitfires of the BBMF since its inception in July 1957. However, in all that time only two non-Western European squadrons have had their markings represented, and both are featured in this May 1994 shot taken on a hazy day over Lincolnshire. In the foreground PZ865 models the highly original scheme adopted by the Flight in the previous year to honour those who served in the Mediterranean theatre with the Middle East Air Force. Wearing the code letter 'J', this machine is identical in appearance to Hurricane Mk I P3731 of No 261 Sqn, which was one of 12 Hawker fighters flown into Malta in September 1940 from HMS *Argus* to mark the start of Operation *Hurry*. Formating with the Hurricane is the sleek Spitfire Mk XIX PM631, sprayed up in the colours of a Mk XIV of No XI Sqn whilst serving in Burma with South-East Asia Command in June 1945. By coincidence, No XI Sqn's previous equipment prior to converting onto the Spitfire XIV had been the venerable Hurricane IIc – the unit had only made the swap a mere three months before VJ Day *(Duncan Cubitt)*

Above Rarely getting into the photographer's frame along with the Spitfire and Hurricane, the BBMF's flagship, Lancaster B.I PA474, enjoys a brief moment of formation flying with its 'escorts' before breaking off back into the landing pattern at Coningsby. Like many of the Flight's aircraft, the Lancaster has recently had its markings modified to represent a No 9 Sqn machine as flown in 1944 (*Duncan Cubitt*)

LF363 – A Phoenix Rising

In August 1994 the Ministry of Defence (MoD) announced, after much speculation within the warbird fraternity, that the Battle of Britain Memorial Flight's wrecked Hurricane Mk IIc would finally be rebuilt three years after it had been virtually written off in a forced landing at RAF Wittering on 11 September 1991. The winners of the contract to restore LF363 were Historic Flying Ltd of Audley End, Essex, an outfit better known for their quality Spitfire restorations.

Since the company's foundation in 1988, following Managing Director Tim Routsis' history-making deal with the MoD to acquire five ex-RAF gate guard Spitfires for restoration to airworthiness, Historic Flying has returned more examples of Supermarine's legendary fighter to the skies than any other rebuilder the world over – they recently started their eleventh restoration. Known for both the quality of their work and its punctual delivery, Historic Flying are now broadening their rebuilding base to include non-stressed skin designs, with the Hurricane perhaps being the ultimate British example of the 'wood and stringers' design philosophy.

One of the founding members of the company is Clive Denney, a co-director and one of the best fabric specialists in Britain. In the following interview, conducted specifically for this book in November 1994, Clive talks openly about Historic Flying's restoration techniques, and how they are to be applied to the rebuilding of LF363.

'We tendered for the contract for the rebuild of Hurricane IIc LF363 along with several other companies, and although we knew that our bid had been successful late in 1993, we didn't announce it because we weren't sure that funds were going to made available to allow the restoration to go ahead. For months there was a continual stream of on/off, on/off rumours emanating from within the MoD, and I personally just couldn't believe that they were going to go ahead with it until the charred remains of the aircraft actually arrived here on an RAF low-loader in the late summer of 1994.

Above Looking hauntingly similar to the shocking post-Blitzkrieg photographs of Schaffen-Diest airfield in Belgium, following the Luftwaffe's surprise raids of 10 May 1940 which left three Hurricanes totally destroyed and six badly damaged, LF363 sits forlornly on the Wittering runway. What had started out on 11 September 1991 as a simple cross-country flight from Coningsby to Jersey soon turned into the ultimate nightmare for seasoned pilot Sqn Ldr Alan Martin when a sinking oil pressure gauge and rising glycol temperature gauge spelt major engine failure barely half an hour into the trip. As the Merlin spluttered and a thin wisp of ever darkening smoke began to emanate from beneath the engine cowling, Martin knew he had to get down fast. He imm-

ediately diverted to the RAF's Harrier base at Wittering, calling an emergency as he slowly lost height. As the pilot approached the runway the fire raging within the engine compartment immediately ahead of him grew much worse, severely hampering his vision. Unable to land into the prevailing wind, and being forced to side-slip in order to see the runway, he put the Hurricane down with its gear up, the burning fighter eventually screeching to a halt in the centre of the tarmac. Fortunately, Martin managed to scramble clear of the blaze, although he suffered leg injuries during the forced landing. The flames were soon doused by Wittering's fire crew, but not before the once pristine Hurricane had been reduced a blackened wreck *(via Aeroplane)*

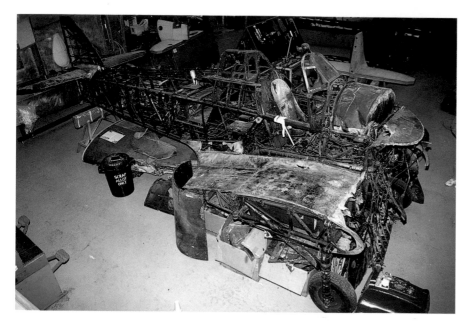

'We won't start hands-on restoration of the airframe until the New Year, so we are currently using this "free time" to get as many blue-printed drawings together as we can, collate this material and then transfer it onto computer. The preparation of jigs is also underway, as of course all the main component restoration on the airframe will have to be built up using this form of construction.

'The Hurricane wasn't exactly an aeroplane built in small numbers, so it was surprising that we ran in to such difficulties initially when it came to tracking down drawings. However, as we got talking to other people in the business, we slowly acquired plans from a wide variety of sources. We have now got to the stage where we have literally thousands of drawings, all of which are being transferred onto computer discs so as to allow us to have a fully computerised analysis of the aircraft, which will serve as a back-up to the originals.

'Historic Flying Ltd have always prided themselves on being very computed-minded when it comes to embracing new technology in the field of aircraft restoration, this philosophy coming from the main driving force behind the company, Tim Routsis, who is an expert in computer technology. I would like to think that in future years the information we have collated and transferred onto computer on the Hurricane will be open for anybody to access, thus perhaps allowing more aircraft to be restored to airworthiness.

'On the topic of helping each other in the restoration business, we initially encountered a fair amount of rivalry from other more established

Right The extent of the damage sustained by LF363 on 11 September 1991 is plainly obvious from all these shots taken at Audley End. However, this angle, more than any other, gives you a good idea as to why a restoration project is considered feasible – the central wing spars of the aircraft appear to have been virtually undamaged in the crash and subsequent fire. Similarly, the steel and duralumin longeron and strut central fuselage section also appears to be intact, although the possibility of it having been twisted in the crash had yet to be determined as this book went to press *(John Dibbs)*

rebuilders when we set up shop six years ago. However, since then the quality of our work has squared the pitch a hell of a lot, to the point where I'd like to think that we can ring virtually anyone in the business and ask them if we can borrow so and so, and likewise if they call us we can reciprocate the favour. There is still the traditional banter of who's going to produce the best, or the fastest, aeroplane, but at the end of the day we are all doing the same job, so why not help each other out occasionally.

'This machine is going to present us with plenty of challenges due to its tubular frame, wood and fabric construction. My wife Linda and I we are the only people here who do wood and fabric, and to be honest with you I don't get called on to do that much wood with the virtually all-metal Spitfire. However, the MoD are supplying the wood to size, so in essence we are fitting it rather than making it. I don't think our engineering team will have any problems systems-wise as the Hurricane's hydraulics and pneumatics are near-identical to those fitted in the Spitfire. Overall, I think the boys will just have to think of things in slightly slower terms with the Hurricane.

'We are talking about pre-war Hawker engineering here of course, which has a wonderfully romantic feeling to it that no rebuilder could fail to fall in love with. I felt this when I worked with Paul Mercer – who has recently left us to join Hawker Resorations – on Stephen Grey's Hurricane at Duxford in 1988. You get a similar feeling with the Spitfire, but to me the Hurricane really is unbeatable for job satisfaction.

'Simply put, we've been in business since 1988, and here at our purpose-

Left With the cause of the crash having long since parted company with the fuselage, the remnants of the firewall and the solid wing centre section carry through spar are clearly visible. The various pipes and cables that transferred fuel, oil, glycol and other sundry items to the Merlin will all eventually be stripped away from the front of the airframe and re-plumbed when the replacement 'heart' of the fighter is finally mated up to the fuselage in 1996. Below the leading edge of the wing in this shot sits the bare framework of the rudder ·
(*John Dibbs*)

Right The task facing the team at Historic Flying looks no less daunting from this angle aft of the cockpit. However, the completeness of the port wing stub is further emphasised here, as is the integrity of the forward fuselage construction. The lifting wing panel has revealed the port fuel tank, an identical item being sited in the same inner wing spacing to starboard (*John Dibbs*)

built facility at Audley End since 1990. Yes, we've worked on 11 Spitfires in that time, six of which are currently airworthy, but I've always thought that the Hurricane was the one I wanted to see in the workshop. Now we've got one – an airframe that is arguably one of the most famous of its type around. Wonderful!

'The airframe really is in a dreadful state, crashed and burnt being the worst possible scenario for a rebuilder to have to tackle. Having said that, you can immediately recognise it as a Hurricane. Yes, its charred and badly damaged, but it is at least a whole aeroplane, minus the bits that have been totally burnt away. It's not a collection of bits in a cardboard box, or a data plate – it's a complete aeroplane. It has come in as complete aeroplane, albeit badly damaged, and it will go out in 18 months time as a complete aeroplane. We have all seen the miracles that were performed at the Cowley Works on damaged Hurricanes during the early years of the war, so in essence, the aeroplane has been damaged and is going to be repaired and put back in the air, with the help of modern technology.

'Obviously, using wartime criterion this aircraft would undoubtedly have been certified as a Category E write-off, and ended up on the scrap heap 50 years ago, but today, its historical links with the RAF – it's the oldest serving aircraft in the air force – dictate that it must be rebuilt, and quite rightly so. This is the unanimous feeling of everybody who has come into contact with the wreckage since it's been with us, enthusiasts and non-enthusiasts alike.

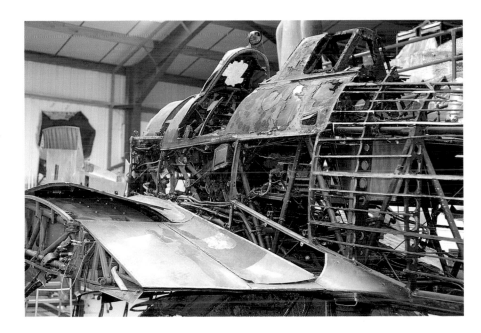

Above The trauma of fire and virtual destruction was many decades away when this photograph was taken at Langley in mid-1949, with AVM Don Bennett's Avro Tudor II of Fairflight Ltd providing an impressive backdrop – note the various primered and camouflaged Iraqi Furies in the distance. LF363 had languished in open storage awaiting scrapping at the Hawkers factory, but through divine providence Air Commodore Vincent (seen here leaning on the propeller) of No 11 Group, Fighter Command, mentioned to Sydney Camm over lunch in early 1949 that he would love to have an airworthy Hurricane to perform ceremonial flypasts with. As luck would have it, Camm knew the whereabouts of just such a machine – LF363 (many believe he was glad to be rid of the weather-beaten airframe!). A fitter was despatched to Langley and the machine was soon made airworthy, although its arrival at the air commodore's HQ at RAF Thorney Island was less than auspicious as the pilot had to belly land the machine on the grass beside the runway as he couldn't lower the gear! Looked after by a series of frontline squadrons until a major refit was undertaken by Hawkers in 1955, LF363 joined several Spitfires at the Temperature and Humidity Flight at Biggin Hill in 1956. Due to the age of the unit's machinery, it soon became the Historic Aircraft Flight, and in turn the Battle of Britain Memorial Flight, and the Hurricane remained airworthy with them until its crash in 1991 *(British Aerospace via Mike Stroud)*

Right Hawkers were very proud of their heritage in the postwar years, and would regularly invite small parties of aeronautically-minded groups over to Langley and then Dunsfold to review their past and present types. This marvellous line-up at the Buckinghamshire factory greeted the local chapter of the scale modelling society in the summer of 1949, a visit which coincided with the near-completion of LF363's restoration to airworthiness. For those modellers not around to see LF363 back then in the flesh, the aircraft was silver overall, with a blood red spinner and black codes (although the codes in this shot may be a matching shade of red as they are barely discernable). Just aft of the cockpit was an air commodore's pennent and a No 11 Group heraldic badge (*British Aerospace via Mike Stroud*)

'The airframe has been barely touched since it was transported from the crash site at RAF Wittering to the BBMF hangar at RAF Coningsby. Several sections of tubing were cut away from the fuselage soon after it arrived back with the Flight for analysis by the Cranfield Institute of Technology, who passed them as serviceable, and having not suffered any weakening due to the crash or subsequent fire. Whether that is still the case now we really don't know. For example, we're currently unsure as to whether the airframe is twisted or not, a fact we won't be able to fully ascertain until we commence the rebuild. I would imagine that the soot and assorted wreckage still on the airframe three years after the crash has had an adverse affect on the overall structure. Ideally, the aircraft would have benefited from an immediate restoration, but financially that was never going to be the case. Having said that, I believe that we will save 50 per cent of the original structure, and with a slice of luck maybe a little bit more.

'If the fuselage is indeed twisted it really won't make a lot of difference because we are planning on re-tubing the aircraft anyway. However, if the centre section has experienced similar damage then that could present problems. We really won't know until we get it into a jig.

'Looking at the overall job before we have cut metal on it, the biggest problems we are likely to encounter in the process of the restoration will occur if we find we have damaged wing spars. We already know that we have one in poor condition in the centre section at the front of the wing – this received an all mighty thump in the forced landing and will definitely have to be replaced. We have purposely left the remaining structure untouched so far in order not to lose information that is a physical part of the aeroplane now.

Once we have completed our jigs and have all the paperwork in order – both tasks should be completed by January 1995 – we will start to carefully

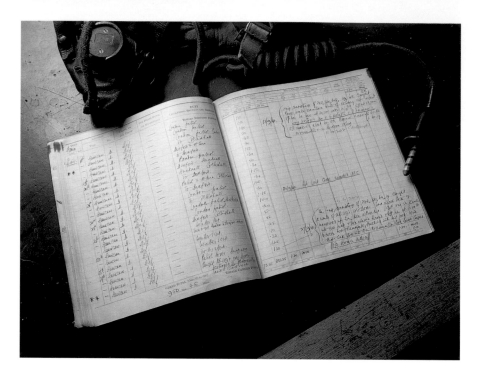

Above and right After almost two decades in basic late war Fighter Command colours (bar a short spell in 1968 when it donned olive drab and earth for *The Battle of Britain* film), LF363 was resprayed in 1969 as Sqn Ldr Douglas Bader's Hurricane Mk I from No 242 Sqn, which he led throughout the Battle of Britain from Coltishall and then Duxford. Approval for this change of identity came from none other than Bader himself, who had jokingly complained at a dinner he had attended at Coltishall earlier in the year that LF363 was still marked up in its fictitious, and badly weathered, film codes. Coltishall's station commander seized the opportunity and asked Bader if the Flight could have the honour of wearing his wartime markings on the aircraft. He readily agreed!

Two Hurricanes were flown by the limbless squadron leader whilst he was with the predominantly Canadian No 242 Sqn; P3061, in which Bader shot down seven aircraft before the fighter was badly damaged in a dogfight with a Bf 109E on 9 September; and V7467, which remained with No 242 Sqn for several months after Bader had been posted to take command of the Tangmere Wing – he shot down 4.5 aircraft with the latter Hurricane. The photograph of Bader's logbook, held at the RAF Museum, describes nine days of consecutive combat patrols in V7467 between 18 and 27 September 1940, during which time he shot down three aircraft, and claimed a probable. Thirty-six years later, the BBMF's 'LE-D' was captured on film cruising over its spiritual home of Duxford, its pilot even going so far as to wear an authentic leather flying helmet to recreate past glories
(Richard Winslade and Mike Vines)

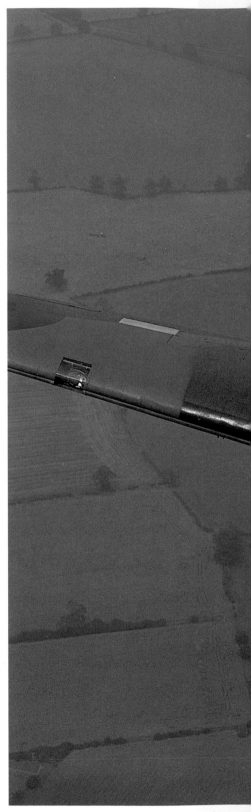

Above and right As with PZ865, LF363 donned authentic Battle of Britain colours in 1989 in preparation for the BBMF's hectic schedule of engagements in 1990. The Flight chose to honour Fighter Command's only Victoria Cross winner of the war when it picked the new scheme, the original 'GN-A' (P3576) of No 249 Sqn having been flown by Flt Lt James Brindley Nicolson. Having only been brought down south to Boscombe Down from Church Fenton two days before, the squadron had scrambled to patrol a line from Poole to Southampton when they intercepted a force of 12 Ju 88s and 18 Bf 110s that had just raided the Gosport naval yard unopposed.

The three Hurricanes of Red Section were detached to engage the enemy, but just as they were about to open fire they were bounced by a Staffel of Bf 109Es from JG 53. All three Hurricanes were hit, with one pilot diving away to safety, a second bailing out but then losing his life when his parachute collapsed, and the third, flown by Nicolson, continuing to dive on the Bf 110s despite being engulfed in flames. After making a pass on the *Zerstörers*, the Hurricane pilot abandoned his fighter and descended to earth suffering burns to his face and hands, plus gunshot wounds to his buttocks after having been mistakenly shot at from the ground whilst in his 'chute by members of the Local Defence Volunteers regiment! Nicolson made a full recovery, only to be killed in May 1945 in Burma when the Liberator he had joined to observe a bombing raid suffered an engine fire and crashed *(both Richard Winslade)*

put five or six tradesmen on the aeroplane full-time in the New Year. I'm not saying that they will be our best engineers, as I'd like to think that all our blokes are pretty much equal in their ability to turn out a first-rate job. We have individuals particularly skilled in sheet metal, or systems or fabric, and the proof of their expertise in relation to this job will be seen in mid-1996 when LF363 is rolled out once again.

'With regards to the quality of the work performed here, this job differs significantly from any other tackled by Historic Flying in that the MoD will send its own inspectors to check the work at certain stages throughout the job, as opposed to a CAA official issuing the aeroplane with a certificate of airworthiness once the overall restoration has been completed. The standard of our work has to pass the MoD's own Defence Quality Assurance (DQA) assessments, which are carried out at regular periods. Marshall Aerospace are the design authority on the Hurricane, so anything that we can't handle here in terms of fabricating or non-destructive testing will be handled by them. Marshall's have in-house DQA inspectors because of the nature of their work with the RAF's Hercules and Tristar fleets. Fortunately, we have already made contact with the chief inspector handling this restoration and he is an "old aircraft" man, so we're on the right footing from the word go.

'Due to the amount of work we are currently handling, we have a number of contractors in the hangar, although the backbone of our staff have been with us for over four years. The workforce is split into teams, with one person controlling the sheet metal side of things, and another the systems. They are not foremans as such, but they are totally responsible to the inspectors within the company. Overall, the chain of authority sees the contractors reporting to the project leaders, who in turn answer to the inspectors, who then submit their reports to the CAA.

'As my speciality is fabrics, I will be responsible for the overall refabricating of this machine, and I have to admit that I really can't wait! In the 20 years that I've been doing this job, the best project I've ever worked on was the refabricating of Stephen Grey's Hurricane at Duxford. That took my wife and I six weeks to complete, and ironically enough this very airframe was also having its fabric replaced not too many miles away at Cranfield at virtually the same time.

'The small bits are tackled first – the fin first, then the rudder, tailplane, ailerons and the elevators. Finally, the fuselage was tackled. This latter stage also includes the fiddly removable panels which fit beneath the centre fuselage. They are very time-consuming to get exactly right, and to me, a job has to be done correctly in time-honoured fashion. The stitching has to be straight, the tapes aligned correctly and the overall fabric made to follow the contour and radius of the trailing edge in one piece, not cut to suit. Fabric work really is a tactile pursuit – I just love the feel of the linen

Above All markings applied to the BBMF's fleet of aircraft are totally accurate in terms of colour and application. This grubby 1940-spec roundel was worn on LF363. Notice the textured finish of the Irish linen, which contrasts significantly with the smooth, flush-riveted, fuselage of the Spitfire. The weight of the two-tone paint applied to the RAF's fighter force in 1938 was much criticised by the speed-conscious pilots on the frontline squadrons, as Pete Brothers explains. 'One of the things we used to complain about at squadron level was the camouflage paint. We didn't think it was very good, or helped our cause very much, and of course it added extra weight to the aircraft. I know that unpainted silver metal would have made us very easy to see, but nevertheless we did seem to carry around an awful lot of extra weight. We should have painted the aircraft in a single shade of dark green, applied in a very thin layer' (Richard WInslade)

Above Sqn Ldr Paul Day makes a fast pass at the rear of the BBMF's Lancaster as he escorts the bomber down to a display in the south-east of England in early 1990. From this angle the great depth of the fighter's cantilever wing is clearly evident, the strength built into the flying surface by Camm and his team saving many a pilot's life during its service career (*Jeremy Flack*)

and the smell of the dope! In terms of difficulty, the Hurricane really doesn't present a problem primarily due to its size – it lacks the many intricate fabricating tasks posed with a small biplane, for example.

'From a finisher's point of view, this project allows me to produce an aeroplane in exactly the same condition as it came out of the factory at Langley in late 1943, utilising the right fabric, stencils and paint scheme. Quite appropriately, the finished machine is scheduled to be re-sprayed in the colours of "US-C"/R4197, a No 56 Sqn Hurricane Mk I from the summer of 1940 – the unit's nickname is, of course, the "Firebirds"! Ironically, this fighter crashed near my home at High Easter, in Essex, on 31 August 1940 after tangling with an overwhelming number of Bf 110s from ZG 26. Its pilot, Plt Off Maurice Mounsdon, landed with serious burns at Great Dunmoor, also in Essex. R4197 had only been delivered to No 56 Sqn at North Weald 18 days before, fresh from Hawkers, and it was one of four Hurricanes from the unit shot down by Bf 110s on 31 August.

'In terms of the actual raw materials themselves, you can buy American-manufactured fabric like Ceconite, which you will find most of the North American aeroplanes are covered in, but I won't use anything other than Irish linen – unless a customer specifically asks for one of the modern coverings. They covered aircraft from World War 1 in Irish linen, so to keep with tradition, and therefore make the restoration as original as possible, that is what will be used here at Historic Flying.

'If you start using modern materials and methods, which use heat rather than dope to shrink the fabric to size, they may be quicker and easier to apply but in the long run the traditional skills are slowly lost.

'Looking at the Hurricane as a whole, it still amazes me that they could produce that type of aeroplane in bulk, with its labour-intensive fuselage and wing construction, on a production line 50 years ago. Of course at the time the Spitfire was considered to be the type that posed the most manufacturing headaches because of its new stress-skinned, sheet metal, airframe, which challenged the traditional wooden and fabric approach that had been employed by the British aeronautical industry for so long. Sixty years hence, that type of construction has all but disappeared within the aerospace industry the world over, which therefore means that a Hurricane restoration is liable to take at least 50 per cent longer than a similar job performed on a Spitfire in comparable condition.

'Tim Routsis also owns another two Hurricanes which have recently come into the country from Russia, and these will also eventually be restored here. The costs incurred in making specialised jigs for LF363 will therefore be spread over three jobs, thus making further Hurricane restoration work more economically viable. Although the world is currently populated with over 40 airworthy Spitfires, and only five Hurricanes, Paul Mercer and I looked over at least six Canadian airframes in a scrapyard in Hawkins, East Texas, two or three years ago, all of which could be restored to airworthiness with a bit of money. As to ascertaining there individual identities, well that is another matter entirely.

'When putting in a quote for the restoration of this machine we really had to provide an educated "guesstimate" in terms of the hours it would take, and how much it would cost, simply because we had never undertaken such a task before. At the end of the day, we have set a price of around £500,000 for the full restoration, and we have to ensure that we don't blow that figure out through either material costs or time delays. All our material costs and delivery dates are based on a schedule originally worked out for our first Spitfire restoration (Mk XVI RW382), which we

Above There are few finer sights during the warm summer months for aviation enthusiasts in Britain to enjoy than the BBMF's Spitfire and Hurricane combination on the wing. A chance meeting with them as they overfly much of the UK, transiting from one display to the next, cannot fail to set the heart racing. Set against the cool blue/green shades of Bewl Water, in Kent, LF363 and AB910 head for an airshow on the south coast during 1990 (*Richard Winslade*)

commenced in late 1988 and test flew for the first time in July 1991.

'We have made money on some jobs and lost money on others in the intervening period, but obviously we must be doing something right as we are still here, with a healthy looking order book, and reputation to match! Paul Mercer's input – he has done two previous Hurricane restorations – was very valuable at the time we put our tender together, and his knowledge of this type helped make up for our lack of experience on the Hawker fighter from a rebuilding point of view.

'The winning of the contract for this restoration project is like an official endorsement in respect to the quality of the work we produce. We won the job on our merits against stiff opposition from Cranfield, Rolls-Royce and several other leading rebuilding firms, and after six years and over a dozen successfully completed airframes, I feel that we have now been recognised as one of the leading lights in the restoration business.'

G-HURI

Above When looking at the exterior of a Hurricane, it is hard to believe that its smooth lines are actually made up of dozens of wooden stringers and formers built around the steel and duralumin girder fuselage. This conventional Hawker construction technique was described in the following terms in an article that appeared in *Flight* magazine on 12 May 1938, just as the first Mk Is were entering service with No 111 Sqn at RAF Northolt.

'Little need be said of the fuselage construction, which has been familiar for many years, beyond recalling that use is made of circular section tubes for the longerons, this section being turned into a square section with rounded corners at the points where the struts are attached by flat plates and bolts or tubular rivets. The

struts run zig-zag fashion between top and bottom longerons, so that there is no wire bracing, but the struts in the top and bottom panels run transversely, and bracing is by streamline tie-rods.'

Due to this primary structure being rectangular in shape, a secondary structure was required to round the fuselage out, hence the adoption of wooden formers that were attached to the longerons by metal clips, and the fabric carrying stringers. Closely spaced, the latter gave the Hurricane a polygonal fuselage shape, although the fabric rounded this out somewhat once applied. This view shows Stephen Grey's Hurricane Mk XIIa undergoing final preparations before refabricating commenced in March 1988 in the Fighter Collection hangar at Duxford (*Clive Denney*)

Above Several years of dedicated restoration work had gone into this ex-Canadian aircraft by the time that husband and wife team Clive and Linda Denney of Vintage Fabrics began covering the fully refurbished fuselage in Irish linen. A team of Fighter Collection engineers led by Neil Mercer and Peter Rushen had first got to grips with the Hurricane soon after it had arrived in the UK from Saskatchewan in 1983. Although a modest amount of restoration work had been carried out by its previous owners, Gary Rice and Rem Walker, a decision was made from the word go to overhaul every single part of the aircraft, and thus return everything to the original manufacturer's standards. Here, the Denney's trim off the excess areas of linen from the elevators following the completion of the curing process of the dope. Behind them, the mixed wood/metal make-up of the Hurricane's fuselage is clear to see, *Flight* praising this method of construction because it 'allows a greater number of men to be concentrated on one fuselage, as they can reach into the interior between the members of the girder – the stringers, fabric and metal panels are left off until most of the equipment has been installed and connected up' *(Clive Denney)*

Above The overall re-fabricating job took about six weeks to complete, with the doped fuselage and flying surfaces taking over seven days to cure before final painting could be attempted. This machine, like all 1450 Canadian-built Hurricanes, was fitted with all-metal wings, a design trait introduced to British Mk Is retrospectively in April 1939, prior to a full production line being set up at Hawkers in early 1940. The prototype and early service machines boasted all-fabric covered wings as the manufacturer's lacked the ability to produce stressed-skin wings *en masse*. The fabric wing was only an interim measure right from the word go, Camm and his team realising back in 1935 that the advent of a heavier armament fit to the fighter made the use of metal wings a must. Therefore, most early production Hurricanes delivered to the RAF with fabric wings had had these replaced by May 1940 *(Clive Denney)*

Left By July 1988, G-HURI, as the aircraft had been registered, was substantially complete, and had received a single coat of silver dope on its fabric areas. Plans were initially floated to undertake its post-restoration certification flights in this eye-catching finish, but by the time it eventually took to the skies in September 1989, it had been resprayed in No 71 'Eagle' Sqn colours. Parked behind the Hurricane in this hangar view is the Imperial War Museum's (IWM) Focke-Wulf Fw 190A, which was refurbished in the process by the Fighter Collection before returning to its long-term home at Lambeth *(Mike Vines)*

Above and left The choice of markings for G-HURI reflects the fact that no reasonable documentation or photography of the original airframe in Canadian use has ever come to light. Although it was known to have been part of Canadian Car & Foundry's sixth production batch of Hurricanes, built in 1942, and it had been issued with the serial 5711, its subsequent service with Nos 123, 127 and 129 Sqns appears to have passed without notice. Lacking a suitable scheme, Stephen Grey therefore decided to honour the cadre of US pilots who flew with the RAF prior to the arrival of the Eighth Air Force by adorning his 'new' Hurricane in No 71 'Eagle' Sqn markings. The unit had initially formed on Buffalo Is at Church Fenton in September 1940, although the folly of using these Brewster fighters (ordered by Belgium) against the Luftwaffe was fortunately realised prior to the squadron entering the fray. War-weary Hurricane Is were then issued in their place, followed by new Mk IIas in April 1941. Brief skirmishes with the Luftwaffe followed over the next two months as the unit performed Channel patrols from Martlesham Heath and North Weald. Finally, on 2 July a large action took place over France when No 71 Sqn, as part of the North Weald Wing, performed both a Hurri-bomber escort and Circus mission in the Lille area. The first American pilot to claim a kill for the 'Eagle' Squadron was Plt Off Bill Dunn, who shot down a Bf 109F whilst flying Hurricane IIa Z3781 – it is this machine which is today loosely represented by G-HURI. Dunn later went on to become the first American ace of the war, whilst Z3781 finished as the highest scoring No 71 Sqn Hurricane, having a confirmed kill, a probable and a damaged (all Bf 109Fs) to its credit *(both John Dibbs)*

Left G-HURI's office has been authentically restored to its wartime standard, with the small radio beneath the instrument panel being the fighter's only concession to flying in the 1990s. All the operating speed limitations are clearly spelled out in prominent labels above appropriate instruments, thus ensuring that pilots remain within the Hurricane's safety envelope when performing aerobatics. To the right of the pilot's cloth flying cap is the much maligned H-shaped flap/gear selector *(John Dibbs)*

Above Although perhaps not as generous in its square footage when it comes to cockpit space as some of the other types in the Fighter Collection fleet, the Hurricane is nevertheless not as tight across the shoulders as its more famous contemporary, the Spitfire. The ergonomics of the cockpit are generally quite good, although it lacks a floor, being fitted with just an adjustable seat and trays for the pilot's feet to slide on. The sliding hood was relatively easy to open once aloft, unlike the Spitfire, and the Mk IIs all boasted a jettisonable canopy *(John Dibbs)*

Left and above The marvellous contours of fabric and metal that comprise a Hurricane are accentuated in these two views of G-HURI in extreme light conditions. The tautness of the shrunken linen over the stringers gives the Hawker fighter a solid look that belies the predominantly wooden secondary structure of the aircraft. By contrast the all-metal wings, festooned with rivets, give the casual observer a glimpse of what lay in store for all future Hawker fighter designs *(John Dibbs and Richard Winslade)*

Left Stephen Grey hauls G-HURI off the short grass strip at Old Warden during a Shuttleworth display in 1993, the gear already cycling away into the wing. The retraction of the undercarriage is something that has caused several of Grey's pilots anxious moments in this aircraft, the H-selector gate proving an awkward piece of apparatus to operate as the small handle for selecting gear up often feels as if it is in the 'up' notch when in reality it is not! Grey's own philosophy when retracting the gear sees him vigorously 'launching' the aircraft once take-off speed has been reached and pushing the selector handle up as hard as he can into the appropriate slot, thus avoiding the restriction of the safety catch. The gravitational effect of pulling the nose of the fighter up hard also helps force the oleos into the wells, thus resulting in two red lights on the instrument panel glowing to denote that the gear is up. Following the flight, when it comes to recovering selecting gear down is quite a straight forward process when compared to take-off, the gear usually falling down into place as soon as the H-lever is pulled into the 'down' position. However, if a leg sticks, various procedures could be carried out to achieve full gear down, as Pete Brothers explains. 'Sometimes on approach for landing a pilot would get one red and one green light illuminated on the dash, thus denoting that only one gear leg was locked in the down position. To rectify this problem you could try swinging the tail of the aircraft, and thus get the airflow to pull the gear leg down into the locked position. Another manoeuvre to try was to build up speed in the Hurricane and then pull back hard on the stick in a high-g climb to see if you fling the leg down in to the locked position' *(Mike Vines)*

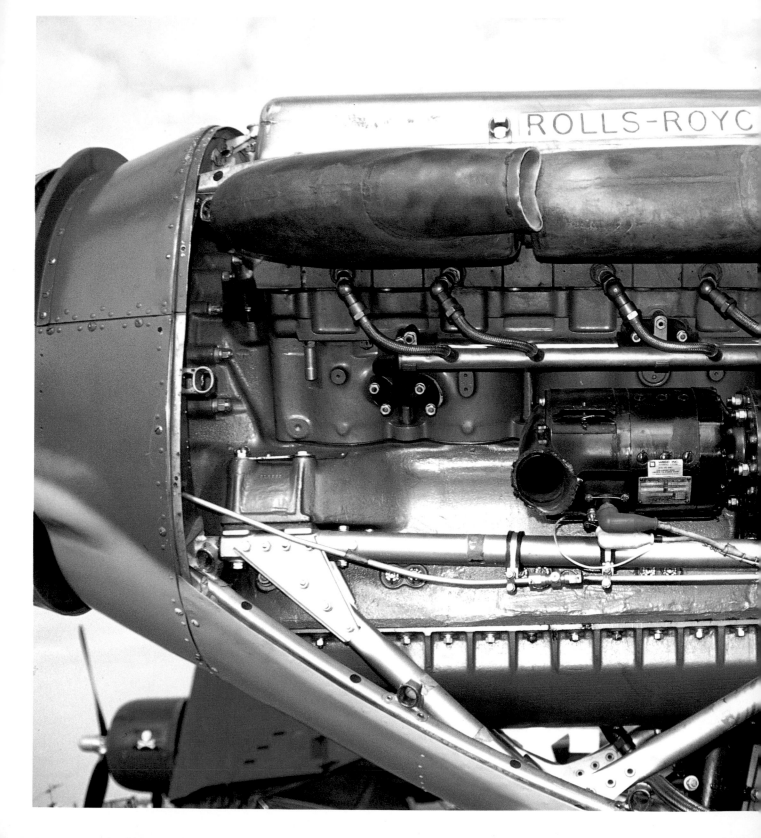

Left All aircraft engines tend to get dirty as they clock up the hours, so the state of G-HURI's Merlin 29 in this close-up shot denotes that the Hurricane had only just passed its stringent air test programme when captured on film. This engine was acquired with the Hurricane in a zero-timed state, and was fully checked out for Stephen Grey by Jack Hovey in California, and only then mated up to the airframe for engine runs in mid-1988. Details visible in this shot include the tubular steel engine mountings, the compact black electrical generator with connected dynamo drive and the early style Rolls-Royce ejector stubs (*John Dibbs*)

Above No problems with gear retraction on this flight, Hoof Proudfoot
having tidied up the aircraft soon after launching from Duxford for this late
afternoon sortie in 1990. Proudfoot, along with BBMF veteran Sqn Ldr Paul
Day and owner Stephen Grey, carried out a fair chunk of the post-restoration
check flying in G-HURI in September 1989. When flying at medium altitudes
at a cruising speed in the region of 200 mph, the Merlin is set at 1900 rpm
with zero boost, the associated fuel consumption in Auto or weak mixture
being about 40 gallons an hour. However, for formation work, as in this
instance with a Harvard photo-ship, the pilot will have to reduce the speed to
about 150 mph and crank up the revs to 2600 rpm. He may also switch the
fuel mixture to rich, depending on the type of Merlin installed in the fighter,
although engine boost is likely to remain at zero in order to conserve fuel. A
small amount of flap may also be chosen to allow the pilot to get in close to
the camera without compromising his levels of control over the aircraft
(*John Dibbs*)

Right Seen high over the Cambridgeshire countryside, G-HURI is banked
towards the camera-ship by Stephen Grey, the sun showing up dozens of
stringers beneath the fabric of the fuselage. The boxing eagle motif adopted
by No 71 Sqn was perhaps one of the most famous emblems of the war, it
going on to feature most prominently on Capt Don Gentile's P-51B *Shangri-La*
in 1944. Photographic evidence of it being worn on Hurricanes is very rare,
however (*Richard Winslade*)

A welcome view for scale modellers, as Nick Grey dips a wing towards the photographer's Harvard camera-ship and reveals the hard-edged camouflage pattern worn by most Hurricanes during the 1940/41 period, prior to the earth shade being replaced by slate grey. Also clearly visible in this planform view are the taped-over gun ports for the Mk XIIa's dozen .303 Browning machine guns. Two types of wing were built in North America by Canadian Car & Foundry; the 'A' wing with eight guns in a conventional Hawker's style grouped layout; and the 'B' wing which boasted 12 guns, of which eight were sited conventionally just wide of the propeller arc, and a further two per wing were fitted outboard of the landing lights to avoid wing stresses associated with two banks of six guns. Some confusion about G-HURI's ancestry arises at this point as it was built as a Mk XIIa, which denotes its fitment with an 'A' wing, but a quick glance at this shot confirms that a 12-gun 'B' wing is indeed fitted. Therefore, it should technically be designated a straight Mk XII. An explanation of this apparent anomaly is provided by the airframe's rather shady history, as it appears that the wings currently fitted to G-HURI may have come from another aircraft *(John Dibbs)*

Left Up at altitude, and slightly above the camera-ship, G-HURI reveals underfuselage details not often seen when the Hurricane is on the ground like the large cooling radiator and the smaller carburettor air intake. Both excrescences changed very little during the Hurricane's production lifetime, with just the radiator being slightly shorter on the prototype when it was first built. The latter works through a liquid-cooling system, and its operability is vital if the all-important engine glycol is to remain within an optimum temperature range. A series of shutters are fitted at the front of the housing, and these can be opened or closed through the use of lever mounted to the left-hand side of the pilot. Being such a prominent structure sited slap in the middle of the underfuselage, the radiator has an adverse affect the aircraft's handling when its speed is increased. This manifests itself only when the radiator flap at the rear of the housing is deployed, however, and causes progressive tail-heaviness which the pilot clearly feels through forces on the control column *(John Dibbs)*

Above A quick gunnery pass on the tail of the Harvard shows both the layout of the guns and the internal structure of the radiator intake. The fact that four guns could be fitted so far outboard on the Canadian Hurricanes perfectly illustrates just how broad the fighter's wing really is, and reflect that Sydney Camm chose to adapt tried and tested wing spars of bulbous steel polygonal section as fitted in biplane fighters of the same era. Due to twisting stresses being greater in a cantilever wing than in a biplane layout, Camm beefed up the Hurricane's flying surface through building the wing spars into a frame, which is braced and stiffened by diagonal drag members which run in zig-zag fashion between the top and bottom spars. They are bolted to the spars via strong forgings, which are in turn fastened to the spar booms by horizontal bolts. Although this arrangement lacked the finesse of the Spitfire wing, and hence restricted the speed and long-term development of the Hurricane, it served the fighter well in the crucial early years of the war through being both simple to build and virtually unbreakable in flight *(John Dibbs)*

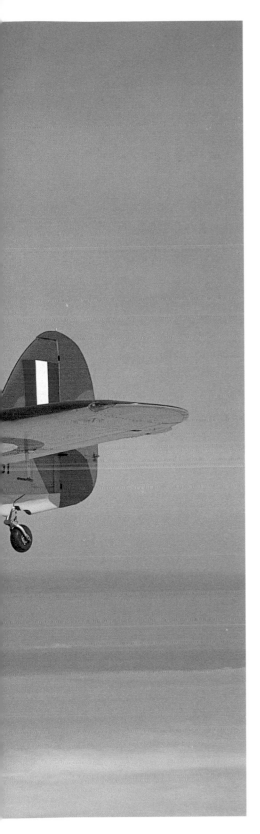

Above and left The only criticism that could perhaps be levelled at G-HURI by the purist is that the aircraft looks far too clean for an operational fighter based at North Weald in the desperate days of 1941. However, that said, respraying an aeroplane is an expensive business and matt paint tends to wear off far quicker than a finish that has been treated to withstand the harsh conditions experienced at high-speed. Equally as important is that a glossy aircraft tends to create less friction as it passes through the air than a draggy, lustreless, machine, hence improving both the engine performance and fuel consumption of G-HURI. Finally, of the tens of thousands that see the Hurricane perform at Duxford, North Weald and Wroughton, amongst other venues, in a year, few would take the fighter's owner to task for having it painted in a semi-gloss finish – indeed, people are more likely to complain that it looked dirty and unkempt if a true wartime finish was ever adopted *(John Dibbs)*

Above Up close and personal, Nick Grey checks the time on the photographer's wristwatch at 4000 ft! The raised lip aft of the propeller boss is an oil collector ring, this device being fitted only to Hurricane Mk IIs, and their Canadian equivalents. The filler cap for the port wing fuel tank is also clearly visible here *(John Dibbs)*

Left With all the shots safely in 'the can', Nick Grey gets the word over the R/T to knock the sortie on the head and recover back at Duxford for a post flight dissection. When flying primarily at cruising speeds and zero boost, the Hurricane has a respectable endurance of almost two hours, which means it can attend events right across the length and breadth of the British Isles, as well as the odd airshow across 'the slot' in Western Europe *(John Dibbs)*

Left Operated alongside the Hurricane at Duxford is the Fighter Collections clip-wing Spitfire LF IXe ML417, which has been restored in the colours it wore whilst attached to No 443 'Hornet' Sqn in 1944. This unit was manned primarily by members of the Royal Canadian Air Force, and had previously existed back in the home country as No 127 Sqn, the one time operators of G-HURI. No 443 Sqn only came into being in February 1944 upon their arrival at RAF Digby, the unit being issued with a batch of 16 factory-fresh Spitfires, including this very machine. It is therefore possible that several pilots within 'Hornet' Squadron may have flown both ML417 and G-HURI (or 5711, as it was known in 1943/44) within a short period of time on either side of the Atlantic. This moody view shows both aircraft up on a 'Rhubarb' over the patchwork fields that surround their Duxford base *(John Dibbs)*

Above Foes of 50 years ago meet high above the overcast in 1990. The 'enemy' in this instance takes the form of the Old Flying Machine Company's (OFMC) much used (and travelled) Hispano Ha-1112 Buchon, which was one of no less than 27 ex-Spanish Air Force examples acquired by Gp Capt Hamish Mahaddie for the filming of *The Battle of Britain* in 1968. Whilst in service with the Spaniards in the 1940s and 50s, the fighter had worn the code C4K-107, and is reported to have served for a time with 7° *Gruppo dc Caza-Bombardeo* in the Sahara. Although not one of the 17 airworthy Buchons that featured so prominently in the elaborate aerial sequences of the film, this machine nevertheless played its part on the ground as one of six used for the ground shots in Spain.

Bought soon after the completion of filming by a museum in Illinois, it was stored for a long time before eventually appearing on the US civil register as N170BG. Far from airworthy, a restoration programme was commenced by its owner, Gordon Plaskett, but before the overhaul had been completed UK warbird owner Nick Grace purchased the Buchon and shipped it back to England in 1986. It finally flew once again on 6 May 1988, and was immediately hired by London Weekend Television to appear in the controversial dramatisation of Derek Robinson's fictional novel, *Piece of Cake*. Sadly, its owner was killed in a car accident in late 1988, and OFMC took on the running of the Buchon from their Duxford base. Since then it has become a firm crowd favourite (particularly when flown by the legendary Ray Hanna) through its exploits of single-handedly taking on a seemingly endless procession of Spitfires during set-piece dogfights at Duxford air displays.

More recently the Buchon has been seen in New Zealand at the growing Warbirds over Wanaka event, and by the end of 1994 it could be found sitting in bits awaiting a well-earned overhaul at Duxford. Its pilot on this occasion was Old Flying Machine operations manager, Mark Hanna *(Richard Winslade)*

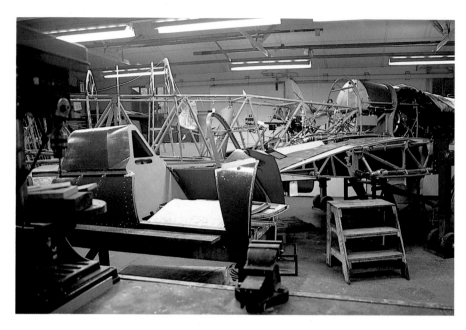

Above and right Although not yet airworthy as this volume went to press, and not technically part of the Fighter Collection fleet, the world's only surviving Sea Hurricane is nevertheless currently based at Duxford, despite being part-owned by the Shuttleworth Collection. As restorations go, the time taken to complete the rework of Z7015 surpasses nearly all previous records for warbird reconstruction – the airframe was initially worked on back in the early 1970s, but a continual shortage of funds has consistently hampered its rebuilding. When these shots were taken at Duxford in early and mid 1988, the primary frame of the fighter had been fully restored, the cockpit section added and the first few formers bolted to the main frame towards the tail of the aircraft. By 1994 its fully overhauled Merlin had been mated to the rapidly progressing airframe and successfully ground run. At about the same time the fighter was resprayed as a Sea Hurricane Ib of No 880 Sqn aboard HMS *Indomitable* at the time of Operation *Pedestal* in the Mediterranean in mid-1942. Z7015 is scheduled to complete it post-restoration flight test programme in early 1995, so hopefully by the time these words are read this hurdle will have been successfully overcome (*John Dibbs and Mike Vines*)

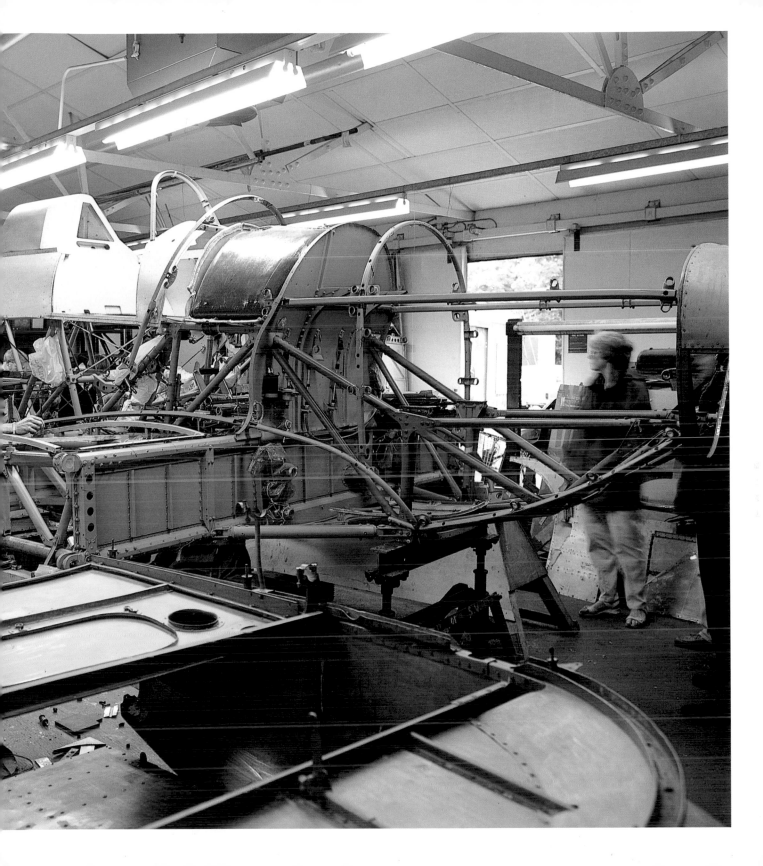

North American Hurricanes

Below Of all the Hurricanes restored to airworthiness in the UK, G-ORGI easily qualifies as having stayed in the 'Sceptred Isle' for the shortest period of time once restored to flying status. Part of the late Charles Church's extensive fleet of aircraft, its future was thrown into doubt following the untimely death of its owner in a Spitfire Vc crash in 1989. At that stage the ex-Canadian Hurricane Mk XII was two-thirds of the way through a thorough restoration at Dave French's Sandown workshop, and it appeared that funding to complete the job may be withheld. However, a US buyer in the form of David Price from the Santa Monica Museum of Flying stepped in and bought the machine at the Southerby's Battle of Britain Auction that was held on 15 September 1990, thus allowing Church's restoration manager, the supremely talented Dick Melton, to press on with the project. G-ORGI duly took to the skies for the first time at Micheldever, in Hampshire, on 8 September 1991, with test pilot Dave Southwood at the controls. The primered Hurricane shared hangar space at Church's Winchester workshop with several Spitfires, two of which are visible in this photograph taken in October 1991 *(Jeremy Flack)*

Above All the flight testing on G-ORGI was carried out with the aircraft sprayed up in this temporary primer/silver scheme. Continual tweaking of the Hurricane continued throughout its brief period of airworthiness in the UK, Dave Southwood complaining initially that the fighter was very tiring to fly due to its heavy stick forces. This problem was partly solved by replacing the four-bladed prop, as well as easing the tautness of some of the control runs to the ailerons and rudder. The Hurricane's hollow construction and multitude of quick release maintenance panels allowed Melton's team ready access to the aircraft's inner workings, thus allowing them to act on test pilot Southwood's observations immediately upon his return to the airfield *(Jeremy Flack)*

Left G-ORGI is fuelled up prior to another test hop. Parked in the Dick Melton Aviation hangar behind the Hurricane is Charles Church's first Spitfire, TR IX G-CTIX, and the primered LF IXe PL344/G-IXCC, which carried out its post-overhaul certification flights concurrently with the Hurricane. The prominent four-bladed Spitfire prop, fitted for the flight tests because a three-bladed unit was, at that point, unavailable, caused Dave Southwood significant handling problems as the increased levels of thrust over the Hurricane's tail unit made the fighter difficult to trim out in flight. Eventually, this makeshift arrangement was rectified and the fighter received its Certificate of Airworthiness *(Jeremy Flack)*

Above G-ORGI was shipped to California in March 1992 soon after it had received its CAA certificate, and reassembled by Craig Charleston at Chino, on the outskirts of Los Angeles, the following month. Here, it was finally resprayed in wartime colours, although camouflage buffs may argue that the shade of green chosen is too light for a genuine Battle of Britain machine! Several schemes were considered, including those worn by Nicholson and Townsend's Hurricane Is during the summer of 1940, before Price finally settled for a No 56 'Punjab' Sqn machine flown by the legendary Geoffrey Page. This photograph of N678DP, as G-ORGI had now become, was taken soon after its arrival at Santa Monica in June 1992. In terms of it pre-restoration history, this machine is shrouded in mystery, having been built at Canadian Car & Foundry between June and October 1942. Reportedly issued to No 125 Sqn at Sydney, Nova Scotia, soon after completion, both its subsequent service and postwar history is uncertain. It eventually appeared in the Jack Arnold Museum in Brantford, Ontario, in the early 1980s, before being acquired by Charles Church in mid-1986 *(Michael O'Leary)*

Above The Santa Monica Hurricane is currently the only airworthy example with exhaust anti-glare shields, a retrofitted item on both day and nightfighter versions of the Hawker fighter during wartime *(Michael O'Leary)*

Left Canadian Hurricanes were completed with two types of propeller as standard, the version fitted depending on when the airframe was built. For example, Mk Is received the de Havilland counterweighted constant speed prop, whilst the later Mk X made use of the US-built Hamilton Standard Hydromatic propeller – the de Havilland version was a British derivative of the

latter in any case. A close look at the stickers on this pristine prop reveal, however, that this unit is from Dowty Rotol, who never provided airscrews for the original Canadian machines. The oil collector ring bolted to the nose of the Hurricane behind the large prop boss is clearly visible in this detail view. The spinner itself has been erroneously sprayed in a sky shade to match the underside of the wings and fuselage. Like virtually most other Hurricane units involved in the Battle of Britain, No 56 Sqn's aircraft predominantly wore black spinners *(Michael O'Leary)*

Above With its Merlin crackling healthily beneath the securely fastened engine cowlings, N678DP taxies out past the rows of private hangars that populate Santa Monica airport. The positioning of the three-letter codes within Fighter Command varied from squadron to squadron during the summer of 1940, some keeping the lettering to a standard size as worn prior to the Battle commencing, whilst others like Nos 32, 615 and of course 56 Sqn chose to apply characters that were in some cases 25 per cent larger than was officially stipulated. This often resulted in both the aircraft's serial and fuselage roundel being covered to some extent by the codes, as in this instance *(Michael O'Leary)*

Above right The Santa Monica Hurricane is powered by a red block Packard Merlin 28 that was zero-houred prior to installation in the aircraft. The cleanliness of this powerplant reflects the small number of hours flown by the fighter up to that point – in the autumn of 1994 the Merlin was removed from the airframe due to a main bearing problem. The most populous piston engine the world has ever seen, no less than 168,040 Merlins were built, 55,523 of them by Packard under licence *(Michael O'Leary)*

Right The quality of the paint finish on this machine complements the restoration work carried out by Dick Melton and his team back in the UK. Note how the code on the left hand side butts up perfectly alongside the blue circle of the roundel just as the original did over five decades ago *(Michael O'Leary)*

Above The Hurricane's hood was a sturdy, if somewhat over framed, piece of
kit that posed the pilot few problems when opened and closed in flight or on
the ground. Most Hurricane owners today have imposed a 150-knot ceiling
on the opening of canopies in flight. The Plexiglas panel closest to the front of
the canopy has been modified to hinge open when on the ground on most of
today's Hurricanes, and this particular machine is no exception
(Michael O'Leary)

Above The authentic personal and kill markings painted beneath the cockpit of this machine denote Geoffrey Page's two-and-a-third kills scored whilst flying Hurricane Is with No 56 Sqn in July 1940. One-and-a-third of these were achieved whilst flying P2970, and consisted of a Bf 109E-1 of 9./JG 51 (the pilot of this machine actually nursed his aircraft back to France, where it was assessed as having suffered damage to 60 per cent of its airframe), which Page mis-identified as a He 113, on 13 July, and a third of a kill against a Ju 88 recce-bomber from 4(F)/122, which was shot down by Blue Section on the morning of 20 July. His only other kill during the Battle was a Ju 87 from 11./LG 1 which he shot down off Dover on 25 July whilst flying P3554. Page's modern day equivalent, owner David Price, appears to have got a little confused when it came to attaching his rank tabs to his overall epaulettes! *(Michael O'Leary)*

Right The original P2970 came to a fiery end on the afternoon of 12 August 1940 following an unsuccessful attack by Geoffrey Page on a well drilled formation of KG 2 Do 17s heading for the Medway towns. Hit ten miles out from Margate having scrambled from Rochford, near Southend, Page stayed with the stricken aircraft for as long as he could before bailing out two miles of Epple Bay. Having suffered terrible burns to his hands and face, he struggled to keep afloat, but was fortunately rescued by the Margate lifeboat soon after landing in the Channel. He was to spend the next two years in hospital having his injuries treated. Cruising over topography vastly different in appearance from that which Geoffrey Page stubbornly defended over 50 years ago, 'P2970' forms up with the photographer's P-51 photo-ship in August 1992. This machine is a welcome addition to the growing ranks of warbirds from the Empire now flying in the USA
(Michael O'Leary)

Above and right A former US Navy pilot, David Price has collected an enviable 'squadron' of historic warbirds from around the globe at his Santa Monica base, his two RAF types being amongst his favourites. The Hurricane was in fact bought by Price to complement his British fighter stable, having previously bought Spitfire FR XIVe NH579 in the UK in 1985, and HF IXc/e MA793 in South Africa soon afterwards. The FR XIVe had been found in India by the late Ormond Haydon-Baillie in 1977 and was duly shipped to Britain along with six other Spitfires. After Baillie's death, it was sold to A and K Wickenden and restored for them by Craig Charleston, and made its first flight as G-MXIV in 1983. Keith Wickenden was killed in the crash of a de Havilland Dove soon after, and the Spitfire was sold to David Price. Museum of Flying Restoration Facility director Bruce Lockwood is flying wingman in the Spitfire in both shots *(Michael O'Leary)*

Above At first glance this suitably weathered Hurricane looks just like any another 1940-period Hawker fighter taxying out to scramble in defence of the UK. However, the presence of a hastily added civil registration on the rear fuselage quickly gives the game away, as do the high-tension wires in the distance. This suitably weathered ex-Canadian Hurricane Mk XII was actually photographed during the summer of 1968 when it participated in the Saltzman and Fisz epic for United Artists, *The Battle of Britain*. For several months the machine joined forces with the Battle of Britain Memorial Flight's Mk IIc LF363 and

Hawker Siddeley's Mk IIc PZ865 in representing aircraft from a fictitious Polish squadron. Formerly registered CF-SMI whilst briefly airworthy in Canada with Bob Diemert, it was bought by Spitfire Productions on behalf of Universal Studios and shipped to the UK in 1967, appearing on the British civil register as G-AWLW, before going on to wear the spurious code 'MI-P' in the film itself. After completing the aerial sequences in late September on the French Mediterranean coast, the machine was flown back to the UK and sold to Tony Samuelson at Elstree (*via Aeroplane*)

Above Whilst owned by Samuelson, the Hurricane was hangared with a pair of two-seater Spitfires (G-AVAV and G-AWGB). Soon after receiving its certificate of airworthiness in May 1969, it was purchased, along with both Spitfires, by Sir William Roberts to serve as the nucleus for his Strathallan Collection. Temporarily based at Shoreham, in Sussex, the fighter was trucked up to Strathallan in March 1972 for restoration to flying condition. Work was completed within 12 months, and on 28 June 1973 British Aerospace test pilot Duncan Simpson successfully flew the Hurricane on its first test flight. During the overhaul it was resprayed as P3308 'UP-A', a Mk I of No 605 'County of Warwick Sqn flown by Acting

Sqn Ldr Archie McKellar. A 5 ft 3 in Scot of slight stature, McKellar was nevertheless a fearless pilot, having scored 17 kills (including four Bf 109s from 5./JG 27 in one sortie) and three shared by the time of his death on 1 November 1940. No less than 13.5 kills and four probables were claimed by the Scot in P3308 between 15 August and 7 October. In fact the aeroplane actually outlasted the pilot as McKellar's favourite Hurricane stayed on with No 605 Sqn until it was replaced by a Mk IIa in January 1941 – he was flying V7609 when he was killed. The 'P3308' of the 1970s and early 80s is seen here, with Duncan Simpson at the controls, taking off during a display at Strathallan on 27 May 1979 (*A Denholm via Aeroplane*)

Right By the early 1980s, the Strathallan Collection was beginning to suffer from a shortage of funds, and its collection of airworthy aircraft was slowly sold off one by one. The Hurricane suffered this fate in early 1984, a buyer being found in the form of the Canadian Warbird Heritage Museum (CWHM), who secured it with an offer of C$450,000. The fighter was carefully crated up and flown back to its country of origin aboard a Canadian Armed Forces Hercules in May 1984, where it soon joined the remaining CWHM fleet at their Mount Hope, Ontario, home. Following reassembly and initial check flights, the Hurricane was re-registered as CF-SMI and resprayed as Mk I P3069 of No 1 'City of Westmount' Sqn, the first RCAF unit to fly alongside RAF squadrons in Britain in 1940. In this July 1986 photograph, the Hurricane is being flown by its regular pilot, Rick Franks *(Michael O'Leary)*

Right The original P3069 was amongst the initial batch of 14 British-built Hurricane Is delivered to the squadron at Middle Wallop, in Hampshire, on 26 June 1940. The aeroplane was immediately issued to the unit's OC, Sqn Ldr Ernie McNab, a colourful character who had been a member of the RCAF as early as 1926, then become a civilian mail pilot in the 1930s before establishing an auxiliary unit in Montreal which would later form the nucleus of No 1 Sqn. He had also served between 1937 and 1939 as a flight commander with the RAF's No 46 Sqn, flying Gauntlet IIs. McNab then returned to Canada to take charge of the RCAF's first Hurricane Detachment in Vancouver, before assuming command of No 1 Sqn in November 1939. Following intensive work-ups, he sailed with the squadron to Britain in the spring of 1940, and when the squadron was posted to Croydon, McNab was briefly seconded to No 111 Sqn, who were also based there, to gain combat experience. Here, he claimed a Do 17 over the Channel on 15 August, before returning to his unit days later and leading them into battle from the Sector Z station at Northolt.

The squadron's real blooding in action came on 26 August when the unit was scrambled to intercept a formation of 7./KG 2 Do 17Zs heading for Debden and Hornchurch. The bombers were protected by 40 Bf 109Es and a similar number of Bf 110s, although the former tended to protect the latter due to fuel shortages. Therefore, the bombers were virtually left to fend for themselves, and unsurprisingly the attack was repulsed short of its intended targets. The Canadians claimed three Dorniers destroyed and three damaged, although one pilot was shot down and killed and two others force-landed following the attacks on the tightly grouped bombers. McNab, flying P3069, claimed one of the Do17Zs after his first pass, but was in turn raked by machine-gun fire from two other bombers. He quickly dropped out of the melee and bade a hasty retreat across London to Northolt, where he affected a safe recovery. The Gloster-built P3069 was withdrawn from service for long term repairs, and McNab went on to fly V7288 to acedom until it too was damaged in combat in early October. This superb formation shot shows the new 'P3069' in formation with the CWHM's late-lamented P-51 C-FBAU, which was burnt out after an engine failure and crash landing. Off the Mustang's port wing is a Corsair II painted up as JT410 of No 1836 Sqn, flown from HMS *Victorious* in 1945 by Canadian Fleet Air Arm ace Lt Don Sheppard *(Michael O'Leary)*

Above As the Director of the CWHM's flying operations, Rick Franks got to fly the Hurricane more than anybody. He also served as the aircraft's sponsor throughout its time with the Museum. This portrait was taken soon after the Hurricane had arrived at Mount Hope in the summer of 1984 *(Michael O'Leary)*

Right After thrilling crowds with its individual and formation routines with the CWH's Lancaster and the loaned Confederate Air Force (CAF) Spitfire IXc, the Hurricane was tragically lost in a huge fire which engulfed one of the Museum's wartime wooden hangars at Mount Hope on 15 February 1993. Only the fighter's engine survived the blaze due to it being with JRS Enterprises in Minneapolis on overhaul. Such was the ferocity of the conflagration, the Hurricane's tubular primary frame melted, thus leaving the CWHM with little to rebuild. The CAF's Spitfire was also lost, as were an Avenger, Auster AOP.6 and a Stinson Voyager, all of which belonged to the CWHM. It is hoped that 'P3069' will eventually be replaced by another airworthy Hurricane, although a lack of funds may stall the acquisition of such a fighter for some time yet *(Michael O'Leary)*

Sea Hurricane II

1 Fabric-covered rudder construction
2 Tail navigation light
3 Rudder tab
4 Elevator tab joint
5 Fabric covered elevator construction
6 Elevator horn balance
7 Tailplane construction
8 Rudder control horn
9 Elevator hinge control
10 Stempost
11 Tailfin construction
12 Fabric covering
13 Rear aerial mast
14 Rudder balance weight
15 Aerial cable
16 Tailfin aluminium leading edge
17 Port tailplane
18 Control cable pulleys
19 Port access panel to tailplane controls
20 Ventral fin
21 Tailwheel
22 Dowty shock absorber tailwheel strut
23 Fin framework
24 Fin/tailplane root fillet
25 Fuselage fabric covering
26 Lifting bar socket
27 Arresting hook latches
28 Dorsal stringers
29 Fuselage diagonal wire bracing
30 Upper longeron
31 Aluminium alloy fuselage frames
32 Bolted joint fuselage tubular construction
33 Deck arrest hook
34 Arresting hook pivot point
35 Bottom longeron
36 Arresting hook damper
37 Wooden dorsal fairing
38 Aerial mast
39 Upper identification light
40 Upward firing recognition flare launcher
41 Tailplane control cables
42 Fuselage access panel
43 Ventral stringers
44 Trailing edge wing root fillet
45 Downward identification light
46 Radio racks

47 Radio equipment (R3002 and R3108)
48 Parachute flare launch tube
49 Sliding canopy track
50 Canopy rear fairing construction
51 Turn-over crash pylon struts
52 Radio equipment (TR1196 and R1304)
53 Radio equipment (TR1143 and TR1133)
54 Battery
55 Oxygen bottle
56 Hydraulic system equipment
57 Dinghy stowage
58 Seat back armour plate
59 Head armour
60 Rearward sliding canopy cover
61 Canopy framework
62 Safety harness
63 Pilot's seat
64 Seat adjusting lever
65 Fuselage/wing spar attachment joint
66 Ventral oil and coolant radiator
67 Position of flap hydraulic jack (fitted on port side only)
68 Gun heater air duct
69 Inboard flap housing
70 Trailing edge ribs
71 Outer wing panel rear spar joint

72 Breech-block access covers
73 Cannon breech blocks
74 Outboard flap housing
75 Rear spar
76 Aluminium aileron construction
77 Fabric covered starboard aileron
78 Aileron control gear
79 Wing tip construction
80 Starboard navigation light
81 Intermediate wing spars
82 Aluminium wing ribs
83 Front spar
84 Leading edge nose ribs
85 Starboard landing lamp
86 Wing stringer construction
87 Ammunition feed drums
88 Ammunition boxes (total 364 rounds)
89 Main undercarriage swivelling joint
90 Hispano 20 mm cannon
91 Starboard wing cannon bays
92 Cannon barrel front gearbox
93 Main undercarriage door fairing
94 Oleo-pneumatic shock absorber leg strut
95 Starboard mainwheel
96 Cannon barrel fairings
97 Recoil springs
98 Cannon muzzles

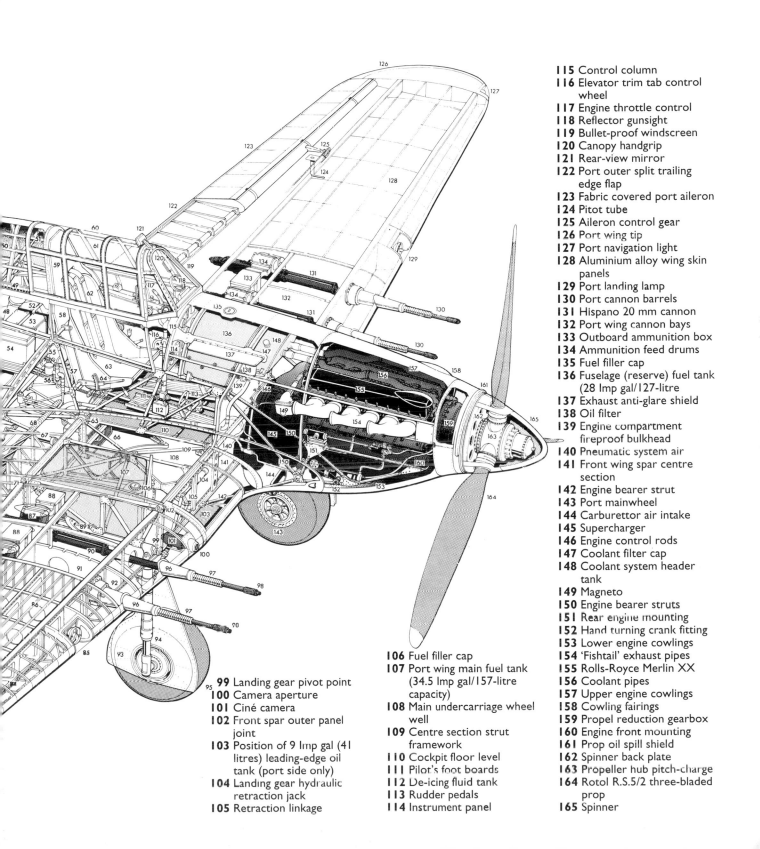

115 Control column
116 Elevator trim tab control wheel
117 Engine throttle control
118 Reflector gunsight
119 Bullet-proof windscreen
120 Canopy handgrip
121 Rear-view mirror
122 Port outer split trailing edge flap
123 Fabric covered port aileron
124 Pitot tube
125 Aileron control gear
126 Port wing tip
127 Port navigation light
128 Aluminium alloy wing skin panels
129 Port landing lamp
130 Port cannon barrels
131 Hispano 20 mm cannon
132 Port wing cannon bays
133 Outboard ammunition box
134 Ammunition feed drums
135 Fuel filler cap
136 Fuselage (reserve) fuel tank (28 Imp gal/127-litre
137 Exhaust anti-glare shield
138 Oil filter
139 Engine compartment fireproof bulkhead
140 Pneumatic system air
141 Front wing spar centre section
142 Engine bearer strut
143 Port mainwheel
144 Carburettor air intake
145 Supercharger
146 Engine control rods
147 Coolant filter cap
148 Coolant system header tank
149 Magneto
150 Engine bearer struts
151 Rear engine mounting
152 Hand turning crank fitting
153 Lower engine cowlings
154 'Fishtail' exhaust pipes
155 Rolls-Royce Merlin XX
156 Coolant pipes
157 Upper engine cowlings
158 Cowling fairings
159 Propel reduction gearbox
160 Engine front mounting
161 Prop oil spill shield
162 Spinner back plate
163 Propeller hub pitch-charge
164 Rotol R.S.5/2 three-bladed prop
165 Spinner

99 Landing gear pivot point
100 Camera aperture
101 Ciné camera
102 Front spar outer panel joint
103 Position of 9 Imp gal (41 litres) leading-edge oil tank (port side only)
104 Landing gear hydraulic retraction jack
105 Retraction linkage
106 Fuel filler cap
107 Port wing main fuel tank (34.5 Imp gal/157-litre capacity)
108 Main undercarriage wheel well
109 Centre section strut framework
110 Cockpit floor level
111 Pilot's foot boards
112 De-icing fluid tank
113 Rudder pedals
114 Instrument panel

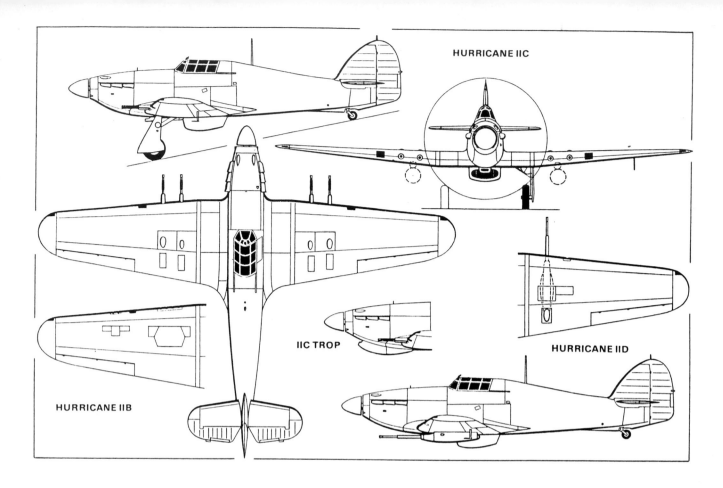

HURRICANE IIC

IIC TROP

HURRICANE IID

HURRICANE IIB

Hawker Hurricane II Specification

Powerplant: One Rolls-Royce Merlin XX liquid-cooled 12-cylinder Vee engined rated at 1300 hp at sea level, 1460 hp at 6250 ft (1905 m) in M gear and 1435 hp at 11,000 ft (3353 m) in S gear. Rotol three-bladed constant speed prop of 11 ft 3 in (3.43 m) diameter. Fuel capacity, 69 Imp gal (127 l) in reserve fuel tank, total 97 Imp gal (441 l). Provision for two 45 Imp gal (205 l) drop or 90 Imp gal (409 l) fixed ferry tank under wings.
Performance (Mk IIb): Max speed, 328 mph (528 km/h) at 18,000 ft (5486 m) clean, 310 mph (499 km/h) with tropical filter; initial rate of climb, 2950 ft/min (14.9 m/sec) clean, 2800 ft/min (14.2 m/sec) with tropical filter; time to 15,000 ft (4575 m), 5.5 min, to 25,000 ft (7620 m), 9.5 mins; service ceiling, 36,000 ft (10,973 m); range, 465 mls (748 km) at 177 mph (285 km/h) clean, 935 mls (1504 km) with two 45 Imp gal (205 l) drop tanks, 436 mls (702 km) clean with tropical filter.
Performance (Mk IIc): Max speed, 327 mph (526 km/h) at 18,000 ft (5486 m) clean, 301 mph (484 km/h) with tropical filter; initial rate of climb, 2750 ft/min (13.9 m/sec) clean, 2400 ft/min (12.2m/sec) with tropical filter; time to 15,000 ft (4575 m), 6 min, to 25,000 ft (7620 m), 10 min; service ceiling, 35,600 ft (10,850 m); range, 460 mls (740 km) at 178 mph (286 km/h) clean, 920 mls (1480 km) with two 45 Imp gal (205 l) drop

tanks, 426 mls (685 km) clean with tropical filter.
Weights (Mk IIb): Tare weight, 5467 lb (2482 kg); empty equipped weight, 6266 lb (2845 kg); normal loaded weight, full armament and internal fuel, 7233 lb (3284 kg).
Weights (Mk IIc): Tare weight, 5658 lb (2569 kg); empty equipped weight, 6577 lb (2986 kg); normal loaded weight, full armament and internal fuel, 7544 lb (3425 kg); max overload weight with drop tanks, 8044 lb (3652 kg).
Dimensions: Span, 40 ft 0 in (12.19 m); length, 32 ft 3 in (9.83 m); overall height, tail down, one blade vertical, 13 ft 3 in (4.04 m); wing area, 258 sq ft (23.97 m2); undercarriage track, 7 ft 10 in (2.39 m); aspect ratio, 6.2:1, dihedral, 3.5 deg on outer wing panels.
Armament (Mk IIb): Twelve BSA-built Browning machine-guns of 0.303 in (7.7 mm) calibre with a total of 3988 rounds in 12 magazines (5238 rounds in some aircraft). Provision for two 250-lb (113.5-kg) or 500-lb (227-kg) bombs.
Armament (Mk IIc): Four Hispano Mk I or Mk II cannon of 20 mm capacity with 90 rpg. Provision for two 250-lb (113.5-kg) or 500-lb (227-kg) bombs under wings.